EMPLOYMENT TRIBUNALS ACT 1996 (UK)

Updated as of March 26, 2018

THE LAW LIBRARY

TABLE OF CONTENTS

Introductory Text	4
PART I Employment Tribunals	4
Part II The Employment Appeal Tribunal	38
PART 2A Financial penalties for failure to pay sums ordered to be paid or settlement sums	56
Power to amend Part 2A	64
Part III Supplementary	64
Schedules	68
Schedule 1. Consequential amendments	68
Schedule 2. Transitional provisions, savings and transitory provisions	71
Schedule 3. Repeals and revocations	73
Open Government Licence v3.0	78

Introductory Text

F1. Employment Tribunals Act 1996

1996 CHAPTER 17

An Act to consolidate enactments relating to [F2employment tribunals] and the Employment Appeal Tribunal.
[22nd May 1996]
Be it enacted by the Queen's most Excellent Majesty, by and with the advice and consent of the Lords Spiritual and Temporal, and Commons, in this present Parliament assembled, and by the authority of the same, as follows:—
Amendments (Textual)
F1. The Industrial Tribunals Act 1996 may be cited as the Employment Tribunals Act 1996 (1.8.1998) by virtue of 1998 c. 8, s. 1. (2) (with s. 16. (2)); S.I. 1998/1658, art. 2. (1), Sch. 1
F2. Words in long title substituted (1.8.1998) by 1998 c. 8, s. 1. (2)(b) (with s. 16. (2); S.I. 1998/1658, art. 2. (1), Sch. 1
Modifications etc. (not altering text)
C1. Act excluded (2.3.1998) by S.I. 1998/218, art. 6
Act excluded (1.9.1999) by S.I. 1999/2256, art. 6. (1)
C2. Act excluded (E.) (1.9.2003) by The Education (Modification of Enactments Relating to Employment) (England) Order 2003 (S.I. 2003/1964), art. 6. (1)
Act excluded (W.) (12.5.2006) by The Education (Modification of Enactments Relating to Employment) (Wales) Order 2006 (S.I. 2006/1073), art. 6. (1)
C3. Act applied (with modifications) (1.10.2010) by The Employment and Support Allowance (Transitional Provisions, Housing Benefit and Council Tax Benefit) (Existing Awards) Regulations 2010 (S.I. 2010/875), regs. 1. (2), 16, Sch. 2 (which amending S.I. was revoked (27.8.2010) by S.I. 2010/1906, reg. 2)
C4. Act applied (with modifications) (1.10.2010) by The Employment and Support Allowance (Transitional Provisions, Housing Benefit and Council Tax Benefit) (Existing Awards) (No. 2) Regulations 2010 (S.I. 2010/1907, reg. 16. (2)(c), Sch. 2

PART I Employment Tribunals

PART I[F2. Employment Tribunals]

Amendments (Textual)
F2. Words in part heading substituted (1.8.1998) by 1998 c. 8, s. 1. (2)(b) (with s. 16. (2)); S.I. 1998/1658, art. 2. (1), Sch. 1

1[F3. Employment tribunals]

(1) The Secretary of State may by regulations make provision for the establishment of tribunals to be known as [F3employment tribunals].
(2) Regulations made wholly or partly under section 128. (1) of the M1. Employment Protection (Consolidation) Act 1978 and in force immediately before this Act comes into force shall, so far as made under that provision, continue to have effect (until revoked) as if made under subsection (1) F4. . ..

Amendments (Textual)
F3. Words in s. 1. (1) and sidenote substituted (1.8.1998) by 1998 c. 8, s. 1. (2)(b) (with s. 16. (2)); S.I. 1998/1658, art. 2. (1), Sch. 1
F4. Words in s. 1. (2) repealed (1.8.1998) by 1998 c. 8, s. 15, Sch. 2; S.I. 1998/1658, art. 2. (1), Sch. 1
Marginal Citations
M11978 c. 44.

Jurisdiction

2 Enactments conferring jurisdiction on [F5employment tribunals].

[F5. Employment tribunals] shall exercise the jurisdiction conferred on them by or by virtue of this Act or any other Act, whether passed before or after this Act.
Amendments (Textual)
F5. Words in s. 2 and sidenote substituted (1.8.1998) by 1998 c. 8, s. 1. (2)(b) (with s. 16. (2)); S.I. 1998/1658, art. 2. (1), Sch. 1
Modifications etc. (not altering text)
C1. S. 2 modified (E.) (1.7.2009) by Ecclesiastical Offices (Terms of Service) Measure 2009 (No. 1), ss. 2. (4), 13. (2) (with s. 9); 2009 No. 1, Instrument made by Archbishops

3 Power to confer further jurisdiction on [F6employment tribunals].

(1) The appropriate Minister may by order provide that proceedings in respect of—
    (a) any claim to which this section applies, or
    (b) any claim to which this section applies and which is of a description specified in the order,
may, subject to such exceptions (if any) as may be so specified, be brought before an [F6employment tribunal].
(2) Subject to subsection (3), this section applies to—
    (a) a claim for damages for breach of a contract of employment or other contract connected with employment,
    (b) a claim for a sum due under such a contract, and
    (c) a claim for the recovery of a sum in pursuance of any enactment relating to the terms or performance of such a contract,
if the claim is such that a court in England and Wales or Scotland would under the law for the time being in force have jurisdiction to hear and determine an action in respect of the claim.
(3) This section does not apply to a claim for damages, or for a sum due, in respect of personal injuries.
(4) Any jurisdiction conferred on an [F6employment tribunal] by virtue of this section in respect of any claim is exercisable concurrently with any court in England and Wales or in Scotland which has jurisdiction to hear and determine an action in respect of the claim.
(5) In this section—

"appropriate Minister", as respects a claim in respect of which an action could be heard and determined by a court in England and Wales, means the Lord Chancellor and, as respects a claim in respect of which an action could be heard and determined by a court in Scotland, means the Lord Advocate, and

"personal injuries" includes any disease and any impairment of a person's physical or mental condition.

(6) In this section a reference to breach of a contract includes a reference to breach of—

(a) a term implied in a contract by or under any enactment or otherwise,

(b) a term of a contract as modified by or under any enactment or otherwise, and

(c) a term which, although not contained in a contract, is incorporated in the contract by another term of the contract.

Amendments (Textual)

F6. Words in s.3. (1)(4) and sidenote substituted (1.8.1998) by 1998 c. 8, s. 1. (2)(a)(b) (with s. 16. (2)); S.I. 1998/1658, art. 2. (1), Sch. 1

Modifications etc. (not altering text)

C2. S. 3: functions of the Lord Advocate transferred to the Secretary of State, and all property, rights and liabilities to which the Lord Advocate is entitled or subject in connection with any such function transferred to the Secretary of State for Scotland (19.5.1999) by S.I. 1999/678, arts. 2. (1), 3, Sch. (with art. 7)

S. 3: transfer of certain functions (1.7.1999) by S.I. 1999/1750, arts. 1. (2), 2 Sch. 1; S.I. 1998/3178, art. 3

Membership etc.

[F73. AMeaning of "Employment Judge"

A person who is a member of a panel of [F8 Employment Judges] which is appointed in accordance with regulations under section 1. (1) may be referred to as an Employment Judge.]

Amendments (Textual)

F7. S. 3. A inserted (1.12.2007) by Tribunals, Courts and Enforcement Act 2007 (c. 15), ss. 48. (1), 148, Sch. 8 para. 36; S.I. 2007/2709, art. 4

F8. Words in s. 3. A substituted (1.10.2013) by Crime and Courts Act 2013 (c. 22), s. 61. (3), Sch. 14 para. 13. (1); S.I. 2013/2200, art. 3. (g)

4 Composition of a tribunal.

(1) Subject to the following provisions of this section [F9and to section 7. (3. A)], proceedings before an [F10employment tribunal] shall be heard by—

(a) the person who, in accordance with regulations made under section 1. (1), is the chairman, and

(b) two other members, or (with the consent of the parties) one other member, selected as the other members (or member) in accordance with regulations so made.

(2) Subject to subsection (5), the proceedings specified in subsection (3) shall be heard by the person mentioned in subsection (1)(a) alone [F11or alone by any Employment Judge who, in accordance with regulations made under section 1. (1), is a member of the tribunal] .

(3) The proceedings referred to in subsection (2) are—

(a) proceedings [F12on a complaint under section 68. A [F13, 87] or 192 of the Trade Union and Labour Relations (Consolidation) Act 1992 or] on an application under section 161, 165 or 166 of [F14that Act],

(b) proceedings on a complaint under section 126 of the M2. Pension Schemes Act 1993,

(c) proceedings [F15on a reference under section 11, 163 or 170 of the Employment Rights Act 1996,] on a complaint under section 23 [F16, 34 [F17, 111]] or 188 of [F18that Act, on a complaint under section 70. (1) of that Act relating to section 64 of that Act,] or on an application under section 128, 131 or 132 of that [F19. Act or for an appointment under section 206. (4) of that] Act,

[F20. (ca)proceedings on a complaint under [F21regulation 15. (10) of the Transfer of Undertakings (Protection of Employment) Regulations 2006] ,]

[F22. (cc)proceedings on a complaint under section 11 of the National Minimum Wage Act 1998,

F22. (cd)proceedings on a complaint under [F23 section 19. C] of the National Minimum Wage Act 1998,]

[F24. (ce)proceedings on a complaint under regulation 30 of the Working Time Regulations 1998 relating to an amount due under regulation 14. (2) or 16. (1) of those Regulations,

(cf) proceedings on a complaint under regulation 18 of the Merchant Shipping (Working Time: Inland Waterways) Regulations 2003 relating to an amount due under regulation 11 of those Regulations,

(cg) proceedings on a complaint under regulation 18 of the Civil Aviation (Working Time) Regulations 2004 relating to an amount due under regulation 4 of those Regulations,

(ch) proceedings on a complaint under regulation 19 of the Fishing Vessels (Working Time: Sea-fishermen) Regulations 2004 relating to an amount due under regulation 11 of those Regulations,]

(d) proceedings in respect of which an [F10employment tribunal] has jurisdiction by virtue of section 3 of this Act,

(e) proceedings in which the parties have given their written consent to the proceedings being heard in accordance with subsection (2) (whether or not they have subsequently withdrawn it),

F25. (f)............................ and

(g) proceedings in which the person (or, where more than one, each of the persons) against whom the proceedings are brought does not, or has ceased to, contest the case.

(4) The Secretary of State [F26and the Lord Chancellor, acting jointly,] may by order amend the provisions of subsection (3).

(5) Proceedings specified in subsection (3) shall be heard in accordance with subsection (1) if a person who, in accordance with regulations made under section 1. (1), may be the chairman of an [F27employment tribunal], having regard to—

(a) whether there is a likelihood of a dispute arising on the facts which makes it desirable for the proceedings to be heard in accordance with subsection (1),

(b) whether there is a likelihood of an issue of law arising which would make it desirable for the proceedings to be heard in accordance with subsection (2),

(c) any views of any of the parties as to whether or not the proceedings ought to be heard in accordance with either of those subsections, and

(d) whether there are other proceedings which might be heard concurrently but which are not proceedings specified in subsection (3),

decides at any stage of the proceedings that the proceedings are to be heard in accordance with subsection (1).

(6) Where (in accordance with the following provisions of this Part) the Secretary of State makes [F10employment tribunal] procedure regulations, the regulations may provide that [F28any act which is required or authorised by the regulations to be done by an employment tribunal and is of a description specified by the regulations for the purposes of this subsection may] be done by the person mentioned in subsection (1)(a) alone [F11or alone by any Employment Judge who, in accordance with regulations made under section 1. (1), is a member of the tribunal] .

[F29. (6. A)Subsection (6) in particular enables employment tribunal procedure regulations to provide that—

(a) the determination of proceedings in accordance with regulations under section 7. (3. A), (3. B) or (3. C)(a),

(b) the carrying-out of pre-hearing reviews in accordance with regulations under subsection (1) of section 9 (including the exercise of powers in connection with such reviews in accordance with regulations under paragraph (b) of that subsection), or

(c) the hearing and determination of a preliminary issue in accordance with regulations under section 9. (4) (where it involves hearing witnesses other than the parties or their representatives as well as where, in accordance with regulations under section 7. (3. C)(b), it does not),

may be done by the person mentioned in subsection (1)(a) alone [F11or alone by any Employment Judge who, in accordance with regulations made under section 1. (1), is a member of the tribunal] .]

[F30. (6. B)Employment tribunal procedure regulations may (subject to subsection (6. C)) also provide that any act which—

(a) by virtue of subsection (6) may be done by the person mentioned in subsection (1)(a) alone [F11or alone by any Employment Judge who, in accordance with regulations made under section 1. (1), is a member of the tribunal] , and

(b) is of a description specified by the regulations for the purposes of this subsection,

may be done by a person appointed as a legal officer in accordance with regulations under section 1. (1); and any act so done shall be treated as done by an employment tribunal.

(6. C)But regulations under subsection (6. B) may not specify—

(a) the determination of any proceedings, other than proceedings in which the parties have agreed the terms of the determination or in which the person bringing the proceedings has given notice of the withdrawal of the case, or

(b) the carrying-out of pre-hearing reviews in accordance with regulations under section 9. (1).]

[F31. (6. D)A person appointed as a legal officer in accordance with regulations under section 1. (1) may determine proceedings in respect of which an employment tribunal has jurisdiction, or make a decision falling to be made in the course of such proceedings, if—

(a) the proceedings are of a description specified in an order under this subsection made by the Secretary of State and the Lord Chancellor acting jointly, and

(b) all the parties to the proceedings consent in writing;

and any determination or decision made under this subsection shall be treated as made by an employment tribunal.]

(7) . . . .

Amendments (Textual)

F9. Words in s. 4. (1) inserted (1.8.1998) by 1998 c. 8, s. 15, Sch. 1 para. 12. (1)(2); S.I. 1998/1658, art. 2. (1), Sch. 1 (with art. 3. (1))

F10. Words in s. 4. (1)(3)(d)(5)(6) substituted (1.8.1998) by 1998 c. 8, s. 1. (2)(a) (with s. 16. (2)); S.I. 1998/1658, art. 2. (1), Sch. 1

F11. Words in s. 4. (2)(6)(6. A)(6. B)(a) inserted (1.12.2007) by Tribunals, Courts and Enforcement Act 2007 (c. 15), ss. 48. (1), 148, Sch. 8 para. 37; S.I. 2007/2709, art. 4

F12. Words in s. 4. (3)(a) inserted (1.8.1998) by 1998 c. 8, s. 3. (1)(2)(a); S.I. 1998/1658, art. 2. (1), Sch. 1 (with art. 3. (1))

F13. Words in s. 4. (3)(a) inserted (1.8.1998) by 1998 c. 8, s. 15, Sch. 1 para. 12. (1)(3); S.I. 1998/1658, art. 2. (1), Sch. 1 (with art. 3. (1))

F14. Words in s. 4. (3)(a) substituted (1.8.1998) by 1998 c. 8, s. 3. (1)(2)(b); S.I. 1998/1658, art. 2. (1), Sch. 1 (with art. 3. (1))

F15. Words in s. 4. (3)(c) inserted (1.8.1998) by 1998 c. 8, s. 3. (1)(3)(a); S.I. 1998/1658, art. 2. (1), Sch. 1 (with art. 3. (1))

F16. Words in s. 4. (3)(c) inserted (1.8.1998) by 1998 c. 8, s. 3. (1)(3)(b); S.I. 1998/1658, art. 2. (1), Sch. 1 (with art. 3. (1))

F17. Word in s. 4. (3)(c) inserted (6.4.2012) by The Employment Tribunals Act 1996 (Tribunal Composition) Order 2012 (S.I. 2012/988), arts. 1, 2

F18. Words in s. 4. (3)(c) substituted (1.8.1998) by 1998 c. 8, s. 3. (1)(3)(c); S.I. 1998/1658, art. 2. (1), Sch. 1 (with art. 3. (1))

F19. Words in s. 4. (3)(c) inserted (1.8.1998) by 1998 c. 8, s. 3. (1)(3)(d); S,.I. 1998/1658, art. 2.

(1), Sch. 1 (with art. 3. (1))
F20. S. 4. (3)(ca) inserted (1.8.1998) by 1998 c. 8, s. 3. (1)(4); S.I. 1998/1658, art. 2. (1), Sch. 1
F21. Words in s. 4. (3)(ca) substituted (6.4.2006 with application as mentioned in reg. 21. (1) of the amending S.I.) by The Transfer of Undertakings (Protection of Employment) Regulations 2006 (S.I. 2006/246), reg. 20, Sch. 2 para. 8
F22. S. 4. (3)(cc)(cd) inserted after paragraph (ca) (1.4.1999) by 1998 c. 39, s. 27. (1) (with s. 36); S.I. 1998/2574, art. 2. (2), Sch. 2
F23. Words in s. 4. (3)(cd) substituted (6.4.2009) by Employment Act 2008 (c. 24), ss. 9. (4), 22. (1)(a) (with s. 9. (7)); S.I. 2009/603, art. 2 (with art. 3 Sch.)
F24. S. 4. (3)(ce)-(ch) inserted (6.4.2009) by The Employment Tribunals Act 1996 (Tribunal Composition) Order 2009 (S.I. 2009/789), arts. 1, 2
F25. S. 4. (3)(f) (apart from word "and") repealed (1.8.1998) by 1998 c. 8, ss. 3. (5), 15, Sch. 2; S.I. 1998/1658, art. 2. (1), Sch. 1
F26. Words in s. 4. (4) inserted (1.12.2007) by Tribunals, Courts and Enforcement Act 2007 (c. 15), ss. 48. (1), 148, Sch. 8 para. 38; S.I. 2007/2709, art. 4
F27. Words in s. 4. (1)(3)(d)(5)(6) substituted (1.8.1998) by 1998 c. 8, s. 1. (2)(a) (with s. 16. (2)); S.I. 1998/1658, art. 2. (1), Sch. 1
F28. Words in s. 4. (6) substituted (1.8.1998) by 1998 c. 8, s. 15, Sch. 1 para. 12. (1)(4); S.I. 1998/1658, art. 2. (1), Sch. 1 (with art. 3. (1))
F29. S. 4. (6. A) inserted (1.8.1998) by 1998 c. 8, s. 3. (1)(6); S.I. 1998/1658, art. 2. (1), Sch. 1
F30. S. 4. (6. B)(6. C) inserted (1.8.1998) by 1998 c. 8, s. 5; S.I. 1998/1658, art. 2. (1), Sch. 1
F31. S. 4. (6. D) inserted (25.4.2013 for specified purposes) by Enterprise and Regulatory Reform Act 2013 (c. 24), ss. 11. (1), 103. (1)(i)(3)
Modifications etc. (not altering text)
C3. S. 4. (1) applied (1.10.2004) by S.I. 2004/1861, Sch. 6 rule 4. (2) (as added by The Employment Tribunals (Constitution and Rules of Procedure) (Amendment) Regulations 2004 (S.I. 2004/2351), reg. 2. (11))
S. 4. (1) applied (1.10.2004) by S.I. 2004/1861, Sch. 6 rule 7. (2) (as added by The Employment Tribunals (Constitution and Rules of Procedure) (Amendment) Regulations 2004 (S.I. 2004/2351, reg. 2. (11))
C4. S. 4. (1)(a) modified (18.4.2001) by S.I. 2001/1170, reg. 7. (2)
S. 4. (1)(a) modified (18.4.2001) by S.I. 2001/1171, reg. 7. (2)
C5. S. 4. (1)(b) modified (18.4.2001) by S.I. 2001/1170, reg. 7. (3)
S. 4. (1)(b) modified (18.4.2001) by S.I. 2001/1171, reg. 7. (3)
C6. S. 4. (5) modified (18.4.2001) by S.I. 2001/1170, reg. 7. (4)
S. 4. (5) modified (18.4.2001) by S.I. 2001/1171, reg. 7. (4)
Marginal Citations
M21993 c. 48.

5 Remuneration, fees and allowances.

(1) The Secretary of State may pay to—
    (a) the [F32. President of the Employment Tribunals (England and Wales)],
    (b) the [F32. President of the Employment Tribunals (Scotland)], F33...
    [F34. (c)any person who is an Employment Judge on a full-time basis, and]
    F35[(d)any person who is a legal officer appointed in accordance with such regulations,]
such remuneration as he may with the consent of the Treasury determine.
(2) The Secretary of State may pay to—
    (a) members of [F32employment tribunals],
    (b) any assessors appointed for the purposes of proceedings before [F32employment tribunals], and
    (c) any persons required for the purposes of section [F36131. (2) of the Equality Act 2010] to

prepare reports,
such fees and allowances as he may with the consent of the Treasury determine.
(3) The Secretary of State may pay to any other persons such allowances as he may with the consent of the Treasury determine for the purposes of, or in connection with, their attendance at [F32employment tribunals].
Amendments (Textual)
F32. Words in s. 5. (1)(a)(b)(2)(a)(b)(3) substituted (1.8.1998) by 1998 c. 8, s. 1. (2)(b)(d)(e) (with s. 16. (2)); S.I. 1998/1658, art. 2. (1), Sch. 1
F33. Word in s. 5. (1)(b) repealed (1.8.1998) by 1998 c. 8, s. 15, Sch. 2; S.I. 1998/1658, art. 2. (1), Sch. 1
F34. S. 5. (1)(c) substituted (1.12.2007) by Tribunals, Courts and Enforcement Act 2007 (c. 15), ss. 48. (1), 148, Sch. 8 para. 39; S.I. 2007/ 2709, {art. 4}
F35. S. 5. (1)(d) and word "and" immediately preceding inserted (1.8.1998) by 1998 c. 8, s. 15, Sch. 1 para. 13; S.I. 1998/1658, art. 2. (1), Sch. 1
F36. Words in s. 5. (2)(c) substituted by Equality Act 2010 (c. 15), Sch. 26 Pt. 1 para. 28 (as inserted) (1.10.2010) by S.I. 2010/2279, art. 1. (2), Sch. 1 para. 5 (see S.I. 2010/2317, art. 2)

[F375. ATraining etc.

The Senior President of Tribunals is responsible, within the resources made available by the Lord Chancellor, for the maintenance of appropriate arrangements for the training, guidance and welfare of members of panels of members of employment tribunals (in their capacities as members of such panels, whether or not panels of [F38 Employment Judges]).
Amendments (Textual)
F37. Ss. 5. A-5. D inserted (3.11.2008) by Tribunals, Courts and Enforcement Act 2007 (c. 15), ss. 48. (1), 148, Sch. 8 para. 40; S.I. 2008/2696, art. 5. (c)(i) (with art. 3)
F38. Words in s. 5. A substituted (1.10.2013) by Crime and Courts Act 2013 (c. 22), s. 61. (3), Sch. 14 para. 13. (1); S.I. 2013/2200, art. 3. (g)

5. BMembers of employment tribunals: removal from office

(1) Any power by which the President of the Employment Tribunals (England and Wales) may be removed from that office may be exercised only with the concurrence of the Lord Chief Justice of England and Wales.
(2) Any power by which the President of the Employment Tribunals (Scotland) may be removed from that office may be exercised only with the concurrence of the Lord President of the Court of Session.
(3) Any power by which a member of a panel may be removed from membership of the panel—
　(a) may, if the person exercises functions wholly or mainly in Scotland, be exercised only with the concurrence of the Lord President of the Court of Session;
　(b) may, if paragraph (a) does not apply, be exercised only with the concurrence of the Lord Chief Justice of England and Wales.
(4) In subsection (3) "panel" means—
　(a) a panel of [F39 Employment Judges] , or
　(b) any other panel of members of employment tribunals,
which is appointed in accordance with regulations made under section 1. (1).
(5) The Lord Chief Justice of England and Wales may nominate a judicial office holder (as defined in section 109. (4) of the Constitutional Reform Act 2005) to exercise his functions under this section.
(6) The Lord President of the Court of Session may nominate a judge of the Court of Session who is a member of the First or Second Division of the Inner House of that Court to exercise his functions under this section.

Amendments (Textual)
F37. Ss. 5. A-5. D inserted (3.11.2008) by Tribunals, Courts and Enforcement Act 2007 (c. 15), ss. 48. (1), 148, Sch. 8 para. 40; S.I. 2008/2696, art. 5. (c)(i) (with art. 3)
F39. Words in s. 5. B(4) substituted (1.10.2013) by Crime and Courts Act 2013 (c. 22), s. 61. (3), Sch. 14 para. 13. (1); S.I. 2013/2200, art. 3. (g)

5. COaths

(1) Subsection (2) applies to a person ("the appointee")—
   (a) who is appointed—
(i) as President of the Employment Tribunals (England and Wales),
(ii) as President of the Employment Tribunals (Scotland), or
(iii) as a member of a panel (as defined in section 5. B(4)), and
   (b) who has not previously taken the required oaths after accepting another office.
(2) The appointee must take the required oaths before—
   (a) the Senior President of Tribunals, or
   (b) an eligible person who is nominated by the Senior President of Tribunals for the purpose of taking the oaths from the appointee.
(3) If the appointee is a President or panel member appointed before the coming into force of this section, the requirement in subsection (2) applies in relation to the appointee from the coming into force of this section.
(4) A person is eligible for the purposes of subsection (2)(b) if one or more of the following paragraphs applies to him—
   (a) he holds high judicial office (as defined in section 60. (2) of the Constitutional Reform Act 2005);
   (b) he holds judicial office (as defined in section 109. (4) of that Act);
   (c) he holds (in Scotland) the office of sheriff.
(5) In this section "the required oaths" means—
   (a) the oath of allegiance, and
   (b) the judicial oath,
as set out in the Promissory Oaths Act 1868.
Amendments (Textual)
F37. Ss. 5. A-5. D inserted (3.11.2008) by Tribunals, Courts and Enforcement Act 2007 (c. 15), ss. 48. (1), 148, Sch. 8 para. 40; S.I. 2008/2696, art. 5. (c)(i) (with art. 3)

5. DJudicial assistance

(1) Subsection (2) applies where regulations under section 1. (1) make provision for a relevant tribunal judge, or a relevant judge, to be able by virtue of his office to act as a member of a panel of members of employment tribunals.
(2) The provision has effect only if—
   (a) the persons in relation to whom the provision operates have to be persons nominated for the purposes of the provision by the Senior President of Tribunals,
   (b) its operation in relation to a panel established for England and Wales in any particular case requires the consent of the President of Employment Tribunals (England and Wales),
   (c) its operation in relation to a panel established for Scotland in any particular case requires the consent of the President of Employment Tribunals (Scotland),
   (d) its operation as respects a particular relevant judge requires—
(i) the consent of the relevant judge, and
(ii) the appropriate consent (see subsection (3)) [F40except where the relevant judge is the Lord Chief Justice of England and Wales], and
   (e) it operates as respects a relevant tribunal judge or a relevant judge only for the purpose of

enabling him to act as a member of a panel of [F41 Employment Judges] .
(3) In subsection (2)(d)(ii) "the appropriate consent" means—
   (a) the consent of the Lord Chief Justice of England and Wales where the relevant judge is—
(i) [F42the Master of the Rolls or] an ordinary judge of the Court of Appeal in England and Wales,
[F43. (ia)within subsection (4)(b)(ia),]
(ii) a puisne judge of the High Court in England and Wales,
(iii) a circuit judge,
(iv) a district judge in England and Wales,F44...
(v) a District Judge (Magistrates' Courts);[F45, or
(vi) within subsection (4)(b)(x) to (xvi);]
   (b) the consent of the Lord President of the Court of Session where the relevant judge is—
(i) a judge of the Court of Session, or
(ii) a sheriff;
   (c) the consent of the Lord Chief Justice of Northern Ireland where the relevant judge is—
(i) a Lord Justice of Appeal in Northern Ireland,
(ii) a puisne judge of the High Court in Northern Ireland,
(iii) a county court judge in Northern Ireland, or
(iv) a district judge in Northern Ireland.
(4) In this section—
   (a) "relevant tribunal judge" means—
(i) a person who is a judge of the First-tier Tribunal by virtue of appointment under paragraph 1. (1) of Schedule 2 to the Tribunals, Courts and Enforcement Act 2007,
(ii) a transferred-in judge of the First-tier Tribunal,
(iii) a person who is a judge of the Upper Tribunal by virtue of appointment under paragraph 1. (1) of Schedule 3 to that Act,
(iv) a transferred-in judge of the Upper Tribunal,
(v) a deputy judge of the Upper Tribunal, F46...
(vi) a person who is the Chamber President of a chamber of the First-tier Tribunal, or of a chamber of the Upper Tribunal, and does not fall within any of sub-paragraphs (i) to (v);[F47, or
(vii) is the Senior President of Tribunals;]
   (b) "relevant judge" means a person who—
(i) is [F48the Lord Chief Justice of England and Wales, the Master of the Rolls or] an ordinary judge of the Court of Appeal in England and Wales (including the vice-president, if any, of either division of that Court),
[F49. (ia)is the President of the Queen's Bench Division or Family Division, or the Chancellor, of the High Court in England and Wales,]
(ii) is a Lord Justice of Appeal in Northern Ireland,
(iii) is a judge of the Court of Session,
(iv) is a puisne judge of the High Court in England and Wales or Northern Ireland,
(v) is a circuit judge,
(vi) is a sheriff in Scotland,
(vii) is a county court judge in Northern Ireland,
(viii)is a district judge in England and Wales or Northern Ireland, F50...
(ix) is a District Judge (Magistrates' Courts).
[F51. (x)is a deputy judge of the High Court in England and Wales,
(xi) is a Recorder,
(xii) is a Deputy District Judge (Magistrates' Courts),
(xiii)is a deputy district judge appointed under section 8 of the County Courts Act 1984 or section 102 of the Senior Courts Act 1981,
(xiv) holds an office listed in the first column of the table in section 89. (3. C) of the Senior Courts Act 1981 (senior High Court Masters etc),
(xv) holds an office listed in column 1 of Part 2 of Schedule 2 to that Act (High Court Masters etc), or

(xvi) is the Judge Advocate General or a person appointed under section 30. (1)(a) or (b) of the Courts-Martial (Appeals) Act 1951 (assistants to the Judge Advocate General).]
(5) References in subsection (4)(b)(iii) to (ix) to office-holders do not include deputies or temporary office-holders.]

Amendments (Textual)
F37. Ss. 5. A-5. D inserted (3.11.2008) by Tribunals, Courts and Enforcement Act 2007 (c. 15), ss. 48. (1), 148, Sch. 8 para. 40; S.I. 2008/2696, art. 5. (c)(i) (with art. 3)
F40. Words in s. 5. D(2)(d)(ii) inserted (1.10.2013) by Crime and Courts Act 2013 (c. 22), s. 61. (3), Sch. 14 para. 12. (2); S.I. 2013/2200, art. 3. (g)
F41. Words in s. 5. D(2)(e) substituted (1.10.2013) by Crime and Courts Act 2013 (c. 22), s. 61. (3), Sch. 14 para. 13. (1); S.I. 2013/2200, art. 3. (g)
F42. Words in s. 5. D(3)(a)(i) inserted (1.10.2013) by Crime and Courts Act 2013 (c. 22), s. 61. (3), Sch. 14 para. 12. (3)(a); S.I. 2013/2200, art. 3. (g)
F43. S. 5. D(3)(a)(ia) inserted (1.10.2013) by Crime and Courts Act 2013 (c. 22), s. 61. (3), Sch. 14 para. 12. (3)(b); S.I. 2013/2200, art. 3. (g)
F44. Word in s. 5. D(3)(a) omitted (1.10.2013) by virtue of Crime and Courts Act 2013 (c. 22), s. 61. (3), Sch. 14 para. 12. (3)(c); S.I. 2013/2200, art. 3. (g)
F45. S. 5. D(3)(a)(vi) and word inserted (1.10.2013) by Crime and Courts Act 2013 (c. 22), s. 61. (3), Sch. 14 para. 12. (3)(c); S.I. 2013/2200, art. 3. (g)
F46. Word in s. 5. D(4)(a)(v) omitted (1.10.2013) by virtue of Crime and Courts Act 2013 (c. 22), s. 61. (3), Sch. 14 para. 12. (4); S.I. 2013/2200, art. 3. (g)
F47. S. 5. D(4)(a)(vii) and word inserted (1.10.2013) by Crime and Courts Act 2013 (c. 22), s. 61. (3), Sch. 14 para. 12. (4); S.I. 2013/2200, art. 3. (g)
F48. Words in s. 5. D(4)(b)(i) inserted (1.10.2013) by Crime and Courts Act 2013 (c. 22), s. 61. (3), Sch. 14 para. 12. (5); S.I. 2013/2200, art. 3. (g)
F49. S. 5. D(4)(b)(ia) inserted (1.10.2013) by Crime and Courts Act 2013 (c. 22), s. 61. (3), Sch. 14 para. 12. (6); S.I. 2013/2200, art. 3. (g)
F50. Word in s. 5. D(4)(b)(viii) omitted (1.10.2013) by virtue of Crime and Courts Act 2013 (c. 22), s. 61. (3), Sch. 14 para. 12. (7); S.I. 2013/2200, art. 3. (g)
F51. S. 5. D(4)(b)(x)-(xvi) inserted (1.10.2013) by Crime and Courts Act 2013 (c. 22), s. 61. (3), Sch. 14 para. 12. (7); S.I. 2013/2200, art. 3. (g)

Procedure

6 Conduct of hearings.

(1) A person may appear before an [F52employment tribunals] in person or be represented by—
   (a) counsel or a solicitor,
   (b) a representative of a trade union or an employers' association, or
   (c) any other person whom he desires to represent him.
(2) [F53. Nothing in any of sections 1 to 15 of and schedule 1 to the Arbitration (Scotland) Act 2010 or] [F54. Part I of the Arbitration Act 1996] [F55does not apply] [F55applies] to any proceedings before an [F52employment tribunals].

Amendments (Textual)
F52. Words in s. 6 substituted (1.8.1998) by 1998 c. 8, s. 1. (2)(a)(b) (with s. 16. (2)); S.I. 1998/1658, art. 2. (1), Sch. 1
F53. Words in s. 6. (2) inserted (S.) (5.6.2010) by The Arbitration (Scotland) Act 2010 (Consequential Amendments) Order 2010 (S.S.I. 2010/220), art. 1, sch. para. 7. (a)
F54. Words in s. 6. (2) substituted (31.1.1997) by 1996 c. 23, s. 107. (1), Sch. 3 para. 62 (with s. 81. (2)); S.I. 1996/3146, art. 3 (with Sch. 2)
F55. Word in s. 6. (2) substituted (S.) (5.6.2010) by The Arbitration (Scotland) Act 2010

(Consequential Amendments) Order 2010 (S.S.I. 2010/220), art. 1, sch. para. 7. (b)

7[F56. Employment tribunal] procedure regulations.

(1) The Secretary of State may by regulations (" [F56employment tribunal] procedure regulations") make such provision as appears to him to be necessary or expedient with respect to proceedings before [F56employment tribunals].
(2) Proceedings before [F56employment tribunals] shall be instituted in accordance with [F56employment tribunal] procedure regulations.
(3) [F56. Employment tribunal] procedure regulations may, in particular, include provision—
    (a) for determining by which tribunal any proceedings are to be determined,
    (b) for enabling an [F56employment tribunal] to hear and determine proceedings brought by virtue of section 3 concurrently with proceedings brought before the tribunal otherwise than by virtue of that section,
    (c) for treating the Secretary of State (either generally or in such circumstances as may be prescribed by the regulations) as a party to any proceedings before an [F56employment tribunal] (where he would not otherwise be a party to them) and entitling him to appear and to be heard accordingly,
    (d) for requiring persons to attend to give evidence and produce documents and for authorising the administration of oaths to witnesses,
    (e) for enabling an [F56employment tribunal], on the application of any party to the proceedings before it or of its own motion, to order—
(i) in England and Wales, such discovery or inspection of documents, or the furnishing of such further particulars, as might be ordered by [F57 the county court] on application by a party to proceedings before it, or
(ii) in Scotland, such recovery or inspection of documents as might be ordered by a sheriff,
    (f) for prescribing the procedure to be followed in any proceedings before an [F56employment tribunal], including provision—
F58. (i). . . . .
[F59. (ia)for postponing fixing a time and place for a hearing, or postponing a time fixed for a hearing, for such period as may be determined in accordance with the regulations for the purpose of giving an opportunity for the proceedings to be settled by way of conciliation and withdrawn, and]
(ii) for enabling an [F56employment tribunal] to review its decisions, and revoke or vary its orders and awards, in such circumstances as may be determined in accordance with the regulations,
    (g) for the appointment of one or more assessors for the purposes of any proceedings before an [F56employment tribunal], where the proceedings are brought under an enactment which provides for one or more assessors to be appointed,
    (h) for authorising an [F56employment tribunal] to require persons to furnish information and produce documents to a person required for the purposes of section [F60131. (2) of the Equality Act 2010] to prepare a report, and
    (j) for the registration and proof of decisions, orders and awards of [F56employment tribunals].
[F61. (3. ZA)Employment tribunal procedure regulations may—
    (a) authorise the Secretary of State to prescribe, or prescribe requirements in relation to, any form which is required by such regulations to be used for the purpose of instituting, or entering an appearance to, proceedings before employment tribunals,
    (b) authorise the Secretary of State to prescribe requirements in relation to documents to be supplied with any such form [F62 (including certificates issued under section 18. A(4))] , and
    (c) make provision about the publication of anything prescribed under authority conferred by virtue of this subsection.]
[F63. (3. ZB)Provision in employment tribunal procedure regulations about postponement of hearings may include provision for limiting the number of relevant postponements available to a

party to proceedings.

(3. ZC)For the purposes of subsection (3. ZB)—

(a) "relevant postponement", in relation to a party to proceedings, means the postponement of a hearing granted on the application of that party in—
(i) the proceedings, or
(ii) any other proceedings identified in accordance with the regulations,
except in circumstances determined in accordance with the regulations, and
(b) "postponement" includes adjournment.]

[F64[F65. (3. A)Employment tribunal procedure regulations may authorise the determination of proceedings without any hearing in such circumstances as the regulations may prescribe.]]

[F66. (3. AA)Employment tribunal procedure regulations under subsection (3. A) may only authorise the determination of proceedings without any hearing in circumstances where—

(a) all the parties to the proceedings consent in writing to the determination without a hearing, or
(b) the person (or, where more than one, each of the persons) against whom the proceedings are brought—
(i) has presented no response in the proceedings, or
(ii) does not contest the case.

(3. AB)For the purposes of subsection (3. AA)(b), a person does not present a response in the proceedings if he presents a response but, in accordance with provision made by the regulations, it is not accepted.]

F64. (3. B)Employment tribunal procedure regulations may authorise the determination of proceedings without hearing anyone other than the person or persons by whom the proceedings are brought (or his or their representatives) where—

(a) the person (or, where more than one, each of the persons) against whom the proceedings are brought has done nothing to contest the case, or
(b) it appears from the application made by the person (or, where more than one, each of the persons) bringing the proceedings that he is not (or they are not) seeking any relief which an employment tribunal has power to give or that he is not (or they are not) entitled to any such relief.

F64. (3. C)Employment tribunal procedure regulations may authorise the determination of proceedings without hearing anyone other than the person or persons by whom, and the person or persons against whom, the proceedings are brought (or his or their representatives) where—

(a) an employment tribunal is on undisputed facts bound by the decision of a court in another case to dismiss the case of the person or persons by whom, or of the person or persons against whom, the proceedings are brought, or
(b) the proceedings relate only to a preliminary issue which may be heard and determined in accordance with regulations under section 9. (4).

(4) A person who without reasonable excuse fails to comply with—

(a) any requirement imposed by virtue of subsection (3)(d) or (h), or
(b) any requirement with respect to the discovery, recovery or inspection of documents imposed by virtue of subsection (3)(e), [F67or

F67. (c)any requirement imposed by virtue of employment tribunal procedure regulations to give written answers for the purpose of facilitating the determination of proceedings as mentioned in subsection (3. A), (3. B) or (3. C),]
is guilty of an offence and liable on summary conviction to a fine not exceeding level 3 on the standard scale.

(5) Subject to any regulations under section 11. (1)(a), [F56employment tribunals] procedure regulations may include provision authorising or requiring an [F56employment tribunal], in circumstances specified in the regulations, to send notice or a copy of—

(a) any document specified in the regulations which relates to any proceedings before the tribunal, or
(b) any decision, order or award of the tribunal,
to any government department or other person or body so specified.

(6) Where in accordance with [F56employment tribunal] procedure regulations an [F56employment tribunal] determines in the same proceedings—
  (a) a complaint presented under section 111 of the M3. Employment Rights Act 1996, and
  (b) a question referred under section 163 of that Act,
subsection (2) of that section has no effect for the purposes of the proceedings in so far as they relate to the complaint under section 111.
Amendments (Textual)
F56. Words in s. 7 and sidenote substituted (1.8.1998) by 1998 c. 8, s. 1. (2)(a)(b) (with s. 16. (2)); S.I. 1998/1658, art. 2. (1), Sch. 1
F57. Words in s. 7. (3)(e)(i) substituted (22.4.2014) by Crime and Courts Act 2013 (c. 22), s. 61. (3), Sch. 9 para. 52; S.I. 2014/954, art. 2. (c) (with art. 3) (with transitional provisions and savings in S.I. 2014/956, arts. 3-11)
F58. S. 7. (3)(f)(i) repealed (1.8.1998) by 1998 c. 8, s. 15, Sch. 1 para. 14. (1)(2), Sch. 2; S.I. 1998/1658, art. 2. (1), Sch. 1
F59. S. 7. (3)(f)(ia) inserted (9.7.2004) by 2002 c. 22, ss. 24. (1), 55. (2); S.I. 2004/1717, art. 2. (1)
F60. Words in s. 7. (3)(h) substituted by Equality Act 2010 (c. 15), Sch. 26 Pt. 1 para. 29 (as inserted) (1.10.2010) by TS.I. 2010/2279, art. 1. (2), Sch. 1 para. 5 (see S.I. 2010/2317, art. 2)
F61. S. 7. (3. ZA) inserted (9.7.2004) by 2002 c. 22, ss. 25, 55. (2); S.I. 2004/1717, art. 2. (1)
F62. Words in s. 7. (3. ZA)(b) inserted (6.3.2014) by Enterprise and Regulatory Reform Act 2013 (c. 24), s. 103. (3), Sch. 1 para. 3; S.I. 2014/253, art. 2
F63. S. 7. (3. ZB)(3. ZC) inserted (26.3.2015) by Small Business, Enterprise and Employment Act 2015 (c. 26), ss. 151. (2), 164. (2)(d)
F64. S. 7. (3. A)-(3. C) inserted (1.8.1998) by 1998 c. 8, s. 2; S.I. 1998/1658, art. 2. (1), Sch. 1
F65. S. 7. (3. A) substituted (9.7.2004) by 2002 c. 22, ss. 26, 55. (2); S.I. 2004/1717, art. 2. (1)
F66. S. 7. (3. AA)(3. AB) inserted (6.4.2009) by Employment Act 2008 (c. 24), ss. 4, 22. (1)(a); S.I. 2008/3232, art. 2 (with art. 3, Sch.)
F67. S. 7. (4)(c) and word "or" immediately preceding inserted (1.8.1998) by 1998 c. 8, s. 15, Sch. 1 para. 14. (1)(3); S.I. 1998/1658, art. 2. (1), Sch. 1
Modifications etc. (not altering text)
C7. S. 7 extended (24.4.2000) by 1992 c. 52, s. 239. (4)(b) (as inserted (24.4.2000) by 1999 c. 26, s. 16, Sch. 5 para. 4; S.I. 2000/875, art. 2 (subject to transitional provision in art. 3))
Marginal Citations
M31996 c. 18.

[F687. A Practice directions

[F69. (A1)The Senior President of Tribunals may make directions about the procedure of employment tribunals.]
(1) Employment tribunal procedure regulations may include provision—
  (a) enabling the [F70territorial] President to make directions about the procedure of employment tribunals, including directions about the exercise by tribunals of powers under such regulations,
  (b) for securing compliance with [F71directions under subsection (A1) or paragraph (a)], and
  (c) about the publication of [F72directions under subsection (A1) or paragraph (a)].
(2) Employment tribunal procedure regulations may, instead of providing for any matter, refer to provision made or to be made about that matter by directions made [F73under subsection (A1) or (1)(a)].
[F74. (2. A)The power under subsection (A1) includes—
  (a) power to vary or revoke directions made in exercise of the power, and
  (b) power to make different provision for different purposes (including different provision for different areas).
(2. B)Directions under subsection (A1) may not be made without the approval of the Lord

Chancellor.
(2. C)Directions under subsection (1)(a) may not be made without the approval of—
- (a) the Senior President of Tribunals, and
- (b) the Lord Chancellor.

(2. D)Subsections (2. B) and (2. C)(b) do not apply to directions to the extent that they consist of guidance about any of the following—
- (a) the application or interpretation of the law;
- (b) the making of decisions by members of an employment tribunal.

(2. E)Subsections (2. B) and (2. C)(b) do not apply to directions to the extent that they consist of criteria for determining which members of employment tribunals may be selected to decide particular categories of matter; but the directions may, to that extent, be made only after consulting the Lord Chancellor.]

(3) In this section, references to the [F75territorial] President are to a person appointed in accordance with regulations under section 1. (1) as—
- (a) President of the Employment Tribunals (England and Wales), or
- (b) President of the Employment Tribunals (Scotland).]

Amendments (Textual)
F68. S. 7. A inserted (9.7.2004) by 2002 c. 22, ss. 27, 55. (2); S.I. 2004/1717, art. 2. (1)
F69. S. 7. A(A1) inserted (3.11.2008) by Tribunals, Courts and Enforcement Act 2007 (c. 15), s. 148, Sch. 8 para. 41. (2); S.I. 2008/2696, art. 5. (c)(i) (with art. 3)
F70. Word in s. 7. A(1)(a) inserted (3.11.2008) by Tribunals, Courts and Enforcement Act 2007 (c. 15), s. 148, Sch. 8 para. 41. (3)(a); S.I. 2008/2696, art. 5. (c)(i) (with art. 3)
F71. Words in s. 7. A(1)(b) substituted (3.11.2008) by Tribunals, Courts and Enforcement Act 2007 (c. 15), s. 148, Sch. 8 para. 41. (3)(b); S.I. 2008/2696, art. 5. (c)(i) (with art. 3)
F72. Words in s. 7. A(1)(c) substituted (3.11.2008) by Tribunals, Courts and Enforcement Act 2007 (c. 15), s. 148, Sch. 8 para. 41. (3)(b); S.I. 2008/2696, art. 5. (c)(i) (with art. 3)
F73. Words in s. 7. A(2) substituted (3.11.2008) by Tribunals, Courts and Enforcement Act 2007 (c. 15), s. 148, Sch. 8 para. 41. (4); S.I. 2008/2696, art. 5. (c)(i) (with art. 3)
F74. S. 7. A(2. A)-(2. E) inserted (3.11.2008) by Tribunals, Courts and Enforcement Act 2007 (c. 15), s. 148, Sch. 8 para. 41. (5); S.I. 2008/2696, art. 5. (c)(i) (with art. 3)
F75. Word in s. 7. A(3) inserted (3.11.2008) by Tribunals, Courts and Enforcement Act 2007 (c. 15), s. 148, Sch. 8 para. 41. (6); S.I. 2008/2696, art. 5. (c)(i) (with art. 3)

[F767. BMediation

(1) Employment tribunal procedure regulations may include provision enabling practice directions to provide for members to act as mediators in relation to disputed matters in a case that is the subject of proceedings.
(2) The provision that may be included in employment tribunal procedure regulations by virtue of subsection (1) includes provision for enabling practice directions to provide for a member to act as mediator in relation to disputed matters in a case even though the member has been selected to decide matters in the case.
(3) Once a member has begun to act as mediator in relation to a disputed matter in a case that is the subject of proceedings, the member may decide matters in the case only with the consent of the parties.
(4) Staff appointed under section 40. (1) of the Tribunals, Courts and Enforcement Act 2007 (staff for employment and other tribunals) may, subject to their terms of appointment, act as mediators in relation to disputed matters in a case that is the subject of proceedings.
(5) Before making a practice direction that makes provision in relation to mediation, the person making the direction must consult [F77. ACAS] .
(6) In this section—
"member" means a member of a panel of members of employment tribunals (whether or not a

panel of [F78 Employment Judges]);
"practice direction" means a direction under section 7. A;
"proceedings" means proceedings before an employment tribunal.]
Amendments (Textual)
F76. S. 7. B inserted (1.10.2013) by Tribunals, Courts and Enforcement Act 2007 (c. 15), ss. 48. (1), 148, Sch. 8 para. 42; S.I. 2013/2200, art. 3. (g)
F77. Words in s. 7. B(5) substituted (6.4.2014) by Enterprise and Regulatory Reform Act 2013 (c. 24), s. 103. (3), Sch. 1 para. 4; S.I. 2014/253, art. 3. (f)
F78. Words in s. 7. B(6) substituted (1.10.2013) by Crime and Courts Act 2013 (c. 22), s. 61. (3), Sch. 14 para. 13. (1); S.I. 2013/2200, art. 3. (g)

8 Procedure in contract cases.

(1) Where in proceedings brought by virtue of section 3 an [F79employment tribunal] finds that the whole or part of a sum claimed in the proceedings is due, the tribunal shall order the respondent to the proceedings to pay the amount which it finds due.
(2) An order under section 3 may provide that an [F79employment tribunal] shall not in proceedings in respect of a claim, or a number of claims relating to the same contract, order the payment of an amount exceeding such sum as may be specified in the order as the maximum amount which an [F79employment tribunal] may order to be paid in relation to a claim or in relation to a contract.
(3) An order under section 3 may include provisions—
   (a) as to the manner in which and time within which proceedings are to be brought by virtue of that section, and
   (b) modifying any other enactment.
(4) An order under that section may make different provision in relation to proceedings in respect of different descriptions of claims.
Amendments (Textual)
F79. Words in s. 8. (1)(2) substituted (1.8.1998) by 1998 c. 8, s. 1. (2)(a) (with s. 16. (2)); S.I. 1998/1658, art. 2. (1), Sch. 1

9 Pre-hearing reviews and preliminary matters.

(1) [F80. Employment tribunal] procedure regulations may include provision—
   (a) for authorising the carrying-out by an [F80employment tribunal]of a preliminary consideration of any proceedings before it (a "pre-hearing review"), and
   (b) for enabling such powers to be exercised in connection with a pre-hearing review as may be prescribed by the regulations.
(2) Such regulations may in particular include provision—
   (a) for authorising any tribunal carrying out a pre-hearing review under the regulations to make, in circumstances specified in the regulations, an order requiring a party to the proceedings in questionF81... to pay a deposit of an amount not exceeding [F82£1,000] [F83as a condition of—
(i) continuing to participate in those proceedings, or
(ii) pursuing any specified allegations or arguments], and
   (b) for prescribing—
(i) the manner in which the amount of any such deposit is to be determined in any particular case,
(ii) the consequences of non-payment of any such deposit, and
(iii) the circumstances in which any such deposit, or any part of it, may be refunded to the party who paid it or be paid over to another party to the proceedings.
[F84. (2. A)Regulations under subsection (1)(b), so far as relating to striking out, may not provide for striking out on a ground which does not apply outside a pre-hearing review.]
(3) The Secretary of State may from time to time by order substitute for the sum specified in

subsection (2)(a) such other sum as is specified in the order.
(4) [F80. Employment tribunal] procedure regulations may also include provision for authorising an [F80employment tribunal] to hear and determine [F85separately any preliminary issue of a description prescribed by the regulations which is raised by any case].
Amendments (Textual)
F80. Words in s. 9. (1)(2)(4) substituted (1.8.1998) by 1998 c. 8, s. 1. (2)(a) (with s. 16. (2)); S.I. 1998/1658, art. 2. (1), Sch. 1
F81. Words in s. 9. (2)(a) omitted (25.6.2013) by virtue of Enterprise and Regulatory Reform Act 2013 (c. 24), ss. 21. (2)(a), 103. (2)
F82. Word in s. 9. (2)(a) substituted (15.2.2012) by The Employment Tribunals (Increase of Maximum Deposit) Order 2012 (S.I. 2012/149), arts. 1. (1), 2
F83. Words in s. 9. (2)(a) inserted (25.6.2013) by Enterprise and Regulatory Reform Act 2013 (c. 24), ss. 21. (2)(b), 103. (2)
F84. S. 9. (2. A) inserted (9.7.2004) by 2002 c. 22, ss. 28. (3), 55. (2); S.I. 2004/1717, art. 2. (1)
F85. Words in s. 9. (4) substituted (1.8.1998) by 1998 c. 8, s. 15, Sch. 1 para. 15; S.I. 1998/1658, art. 2. (1), Sch. 1
Modifications etc. (not altering text)
C8. S. 9 extended (24.4.2000) by 1992 c. 52, s. 239. (4)(c) (as inserted (24.4.2000) by 1999 c. 26, s. 16, Sch. 5 para. 4; S.I. 2000/875, art. 2 (subject to transitional provision in art. 3))

[F8610 National security.

(1) If on a complaint under—
[F87. (a)section 145. A, 145. B or 146 of the Trade Union and Labour Relations (Consolidation) Act 1992 (inducements and detriments in respect of trade union membership etc.),]
  (b) section 111 of the Employment Rights Act 1996 (unfair dismissal),[F88, or
  (c) regulation 9 of the Employment Relations Act 1999 (Blacklists) Regulations 2010 (detriment connected with prohibited list).]
it is shown that the action complained of was taken for the purpose of safeguarding national security, the employment tribunal shall dismiss the complaint.
(2) Employment tribunal procedure regulations may make provision about the composition of the tribunal (including provision disapplying or modifying section 4) for the purposes of proceedings in relation to which—
  (a) a direction is given under subsection (3), or
  (b) an order is made under subsection (4).
(3) A direction may be given under this subsection by a Minister of the Crown if—
  (a) it relates to particular Crown employment proceedings, and
  (b) the Minister considers it expedient in the interests of national security.
(4) An order may be made under this subsection by the President or a Regional [F89 Employment Judge] in relation to particular proceedings if he considers it expedient in the interests of national security.
(5) Employment tribunal procedure regulations may make provision enabling a Minister of the Crown, if he considers it expedient in the interests of national security—
  (a) to direct a tribunal to sit in private for all or part of particular Crown employment proceedings;
  (b) to direct a tribunal to exclude the applicant from all or part of particular Crown employment proceedings;
  (c) to direct a tribunal to exclude the applicant's representatives from all or part of particular Crown employment proceedings;
  (d) to direct a tribunal to take steps to conceal the identity of a particular witness in particular Crown employment proceedings;
  (e) to direct a tribunal to take steps to keep secret all or part of the reasons for its decision in

particular Crown employment proceedings.

[F90. (6)Employment tribunal procedure regulations may enable a tribunal, if it considers it expedient in the interests of national security, to do in relation to particular proceedings before it anything of a kind which, by virtue of subsection (5), employment tribunal procedure regulations may enable a Minister of the Crown to direct a tribunal to do in relation to particular Crown employment proceedings.]

(7) In relation to cases where a person has been excluded by virtue of subsection (5)(b) or (c) or (6), employment tribunal procedure regulations may make provision—

(a) for the appointment by the Attorney General, or by the Advocate General for Scotland, of a person to represent the interests of the applicant;

(b) about the publication and registration of reasons for the tribunal's decision;

(c) permitting an excluded person to make a statement to the tribunal before the commencement of the proceedings, or the part of the proceedings, from which he is excluded.

(8) Proceedings are Crown employment proceedings for the purposes of this section if the employment to which the complaint relates—

(a) is Crown employment, or

(b) is connected with the performance of functions on behalf of the Crown.

(9) The reference in subsection (4) to the President or a Regional Chairman is to a person appointed in accordance with regulations under section 1. (1) as—

(a) a Regional Chairman,

(b) President of the Employment Tribunals (England and Wales), or

(c) President of the Employment Tribunals (Scotland).]

Amendments (Textual)

F86. Ss. 10, 10. A, 10. B substituted (16.7.2001) for s. 10 by 1999 c. 26, ss. 41, 45, Sch. 8 para. 3; S.I. 2001/1187, art. 3. (b), Sch. (as amended by S.I. 2001/1461, art. 2. (2))

F87. S. 10. (1)(a) substituted (1.10.2004) by Employment Relations Act 2004 (c. 24), ss. 57. (1), 59, Sch. 1 para. 24; S.I. 2004/2566, art. 3. (b) (subject to arts. 4-8)

F88. S. 10. (1)(c) and word inserted (2.3.2010) by The Employment Relations Act 1999 (Blacklists) Regulations 2010 (S.I. 2010/493), regs. 1. (b), 17. (2)(b)

F89. Words in s. 10. (4) substituted (1.10.2013) by Crime and Courts Act 2013 (c. 22), s. 61. (3), Sch. 14 para. 13. (3); S.I. 2013/2200, art. 3. (g)

F90. S. 10. (6) substituted (31.12.2004) by Employment Relations Act 2004 (c. 24), ss. 36, 59; S.I. 2004/3342, art. 4. (a) (subject to arts. 5-12)

F9110. A Confidential information.

(1) Employment tribunal procedure regulations may enable an employment tribunal to sit in private for the purpose of hearing evidence from any person which in the opinion of the tribunal is likely to consist of—

(a) information which he could not disclose without contravening a prohibition imposed by or by virtue of any enactment,

(b) information which has been communicated to him in confidence or which he has otherwise obtained in consequence of the confidence reposed in him by another person, or

(c) information the disclosure of which would, for reasons other than its effect on negotiations with respect to any of the matters mentioned in section 178. (2) of the Trade Union and Labour Relations (Consolidation) Act 1992, cause substantial injury to any undertaking of his or in which he works.

(2) The reference in subsection (1)(c) to any undertaking of a person or in which he works shall be construed—

(a) in relation to a person in Crown employment, as a reference to the national interest,

(b) in relation to a person who is a relevant member of the House of Lords staff, as a reference to the national interest or (if the case so requires) the interests of the House of Lords, and

(c) in relation to a person who is a relevant member of the House of Commons staff, as a reference to the national interest or (if the case so requires) the interests of the House of Commons.
Amendments (Textual)
F91. Ss. 10, 10. A, 10. B substituted (16.7.2001) for s. 10 by 1999 c. 26, ss. 41, 45, Sch. 8 para. 3; S.I. 2001/1187, art. 3. (b), Sch. (as amended by S.I. 2001/1461, art. 2. (2))

F9210. B Restriction of publicity in cases involving national security.

(1) This section applies where a tribunal has been directed under section 10. (5) or has determined under section 10. (6)—
　(a) to take steps to conceal the identity of a particular witness, or
　(b) to take steps to keep secret all or part of the reasons for its decision.
(2) It is an offence to publish—
　(a) anything likely to lead to the identification of the witness, or
　(b) the reasons for the tribunal's decision or the part of its reasons which it is directed or has determined to keep secret.
(3) A person guilty of an offence under this section is liable on summary conviction to a fine not exceeding level 5 on the standard scale.
(4) Where a person is charged with an offence under this section it is a defence to prove that at the time of the alleged offence he was not aware, and neither suspected nor had reason to suspect, that the publication in question was of, or included, the matter in question.
(5) Where an offence under this section committed by a body corporate is proved to have been committed with the consent or connivance of, or to be attributable to any neglect on the part of—
　(a) a director, manager, secretary or other similar officer of the body corporate, or
　(b) a person purporting to act in any such capacity,
he as well as the body corporate is guilty of the offence and liable to be proceeded against and punished accordingly.
(6) A reference in this section to publication includes a reference to inclusion in a programme which is included in a programme service, within the meaning of the M4. Broadcasting Act 1990.
Amendments (Textual)
F92. Ss. 10, 10. A, 10. B substituted (16.7.2001) for s. 10 by 1999 c. 26, ss. 41, 45, Sch. 8 para. 3; S.I. 2001/1187, art. 3. (b), Sch. (as amended by S.I. 2001/1461, art. 2. (2))
Marginal Citations
M41990 c. 42.

11 Restriction of publicity in cases involving sexual misconduct.

(1) [F93. Employment tribunal] procedure regulations may include provision—
　(a) for cases involving allegations of the commission of sexual offences, for securing that the registration or other making available of documents or decisions shall be so effected as to prevent the identification of any person affected by or making the allegation, and
　(b) for cases involving allegations of sexual misconduct, enabling an [F93employment tribunal], on the application of any party to proceedings before it or of its own motion, to make a restricted reporting order having effect (if not revoked earlier) until the promulgation of the decision of the tribunal.
(2) If any identifying matter is published or included in a relevant programme in contravention of a restricted reporting order—
　(a) in the case of publication in a newspaper or periodical, any proprietor, any editor and any publisher of the newspaper or periodical,

(b) in the case of publication in any other form, the person publishing the matter, and
(c) in the case of matter included in a relevant programme—
(i) any body corporate engaged in providing the service in which the programme is included, and
(ii) any person having functions in relation to the programme corresponding to those of an editor of a newspaper,
shall be guilty of an offence and liable on summary conviction to a fine not exceeding level 5 on the standard scale.
(3) Where a person is charged with an offence under subsection (2) it is a defence to prove that at the time of the alleged offence he was not aware, and neither suspected nor had reason to suspect, that the publication or programme in question was of, or included, the matter in question.
(4) Where an offence under subsection (2) committed by a body corporate is proved to have been committed with the consent or connivance of, or to be attributable to any neglect on the part of—
(a) a director, manager, secretary or other similar officer of the body corporate, or
(b) a person purporting to act in any such capacity,
he as well as the body corporate is guilty of the offence and liable to be proceeded against and punished accordingly.
(5) In relation to a body corporate whose affairs are managed by its members "director", in subsection (4), means a member of the body corporate.
(6) In this section—
"identifying matter", in relation to a person, means any matter likely to lead members of the public to identify him as a person affected by, or as the person making, the allegation,
"relevant programme" has the same meaning as in the M5. Sexual Offences (Amendment) Act 1992,
"restricted reporting order" means an order—
- made in exercise of a power conferred by regulations made by virtue of this section, and
- prohibiting the publication in Great Britain of identifying matter in a written publication available to the public or its inclusion in a relevant programme for reception in Great Britain,
"sexual misconduct" means the commission of a sexual offence, sexual harassment or other adverse conduct (of whatever nature) related to sex, and conduct is related to sex whether the relationship with sex lies in the character of the conduct or in its having reference to the sex or sexual orientation of the person at whom the conduct is directed,
"sexual offence" means any offence to which section 4 of the M6. Sexual Offences (Amendment) Act 1976, the Sexual Offences (Amendment) Act 1992 or section 274. (2) of the M7. Criminal Procedure (Scotland) Act 1995 applies (offences under the M8. Sexual Offences Act 1956, Part I of the M9. Criminal Law (Consolidation) (Scotland) Act 1995 and certain other enactments), and
"written publication" has the same meaning as in the Sexual Offences (Amendment) Act 1992.
Amendments (Textual)
F93. Words in s. 11. (1) substituted (1.8.1998) by 1998 c. 8, s. 1. (2)(a) (with s. 16. (2)); S.I. 1998/1658, art. 2. (1), Sch. 1
Marginal Citations
M51992 c. 34.
M61976 c. 82.
M71995 c. 46.
M81956 c. 69.
M91995 c. 39.

12 Restriction of publicity in disability cases.

(1) This section applies to proceedings on a complaint under [F94section 120 of the Equality Act 2010, where the complaint relates to disability] in which evidence of a personal nature is likely to be heard by the [F95employment tribunal] hearing the complaint.
(2) [F95. Employment tribunal] procedure regulations may include provision in relation to

proceedings to which this section applies for—
(a) enabling an [F95employment tribunal], on the application of the complainant or of its own motion, to make a restricted reporting order having effect (if not revoked earlier) until the promulgation of the decision of the tribunal, and
(b) where a restricted reporting order is made in relation to a complaint which is being dealt with by the tribunal together with any other proceedings, enabling the tribunal to direct that the order is to apply also in relation to those other proceedings or such part of them as the tribunal may direct.
(3) If any identifying matter is published or included in a relevant programme in contravention of a restricted reporting order—
(a) in the case of publication in a newspaper or periodical, any proprietor, any editor and any publisher of the newspaper or periodical,
(b) in the case of publication in any other form, the person publishing the matter, and
(c) in the case of matter included in a relevant programme—
(i) any body corporate engaged in providing the service in which the programme is included, and
(ii) any person having functions in relation to the programme corresponding to those of an editor of a newspaper,
shall be guilty of an offence and liable on summary conviction to a fine not exceeding level 5 on the standard scale.
(4) Where a person is charged with an offence under subsection (3), it is a defence to prove that at the time of the alleged offence he was not aware, and neither suspected nor had reason to suspect, that the publication or programme in question was of, or included, the matter in question.
(5) Where an offence under subsection (3) committed by a body corporate is proved to have been committed with the consent or connivance of, or to be attributable to any neglect on the part of—
(a) a director, manager, secretary or other similar officer of the body corporate, or
(b) a person purporting to act in any such capacity,
he as well as the body corporate is guilty of the offence and liable to be proceeded against and punished accordingly.
(6) In relation to a body corporate whose affairs are managed by its members "director", in subsection (5), means a member of the body corporate.
(7) In this section—
"evidence of a personal nature" means any evidence of a medical, or other intimate, nature which might reasonably be assumed to be likely to cause significant embarrassment to the complainant if reported,
"identifying matter" means any matter likely to lead members of the public to identify the complainant or such other persons (if any) as may be named in the order,
"promulgation" has such meaning as may be prescribed by regulations made by virtue of this section,
"relevant programme" means a programme included in a programme service, within the meaning of the M10. Broadcasting Act 1990,
"restricted reporting order" means an order—
- made in exercise of a power conferred by regulations made by virtue of this section, and
- prohibiting the publication in Great Britain of identifying matter in a written publication available to the public or its inclusion in a relevant programme for reception in Great Britain, and
"written publication" includes a film, a sound track and any other record in permanent form but does not include an indictment or other document prepared for use in particular legal proceedings.
Amendments (Textual)
F94. Words in s. 12. (1) substituted by Equality Act 2010 (c. 15), Sch. 26 Pt. 1 para. 30 (as inserted) (1.10.2010) by S.I. 2010/2279, art. 1. (2), Sch. 1 para. 5 (see S.I. 2010/2317, art. 2)
F95. Words in s. 12. (1)(2) substituted (1.8.1998) by 1998 c. 8, s. 1. (2)(a) (with s. 16. (2)); S.I. 1998/1658, art. 2. (1), Sch. 1
Commencement Information
I1. S. 12 wholly in force at 22.8.1996 with effect as mentioned in Sch. 2 Pt. II para. 7. (1)(2) and

S.I. 1996/3150, art. 2
Marginal Citations
M101990 c. 42.

[F96. Financial penalties

Amendments (Textual)
F96. S. 12. A and cross-heading inserted (25.4.2013 for specified purposes, 6.4.2014 in so far as not already in force) by Enterprise and Regulatory Reform Act 2013 (c. 24), ss. 16. (1), 103. (1)(i), (3); S.I. 2014/253, art. 3. (e)

12. AFinancial penalties

(1) Where an employment tribunal determining a claim involving an employer and a worker—
    (a) concludes that the employer has breached any of the worker's rights to which the claim relates, and
    (b) is of the opinion that the breach has one or more aggravating features,
the tribunal may order the employer to pay a penalty to the Secretary of State (whether or not it also makes a financial award against the employer on the claim).
(2) The tribunal shall have regard to an employer's ability to pay—
    (a) in deciding whether to order the employer to pay a penalty under this section;
    (b) (subject to subsections (3) to (7)) in deciding the amount of a penalty.
(3) The amount of a penalty under this section shall be—
    (a) at least £100;
    (b) no more than £5,000.
This subsection does not apply where subsection (5) or (7) applies.
(4) Subsection (5) applies where an employment tribunal—
    (a) makes a financial award against an employer on a claim, and
    (b) also orders the employer to pay a penalty under this section in respect of the claim.
(5) In such a case, the amount of the penalty under this section shall be 50% of the amount of the award, except that—
    (a) if the amount of the financial award is less than £200, the amount of the penalty shall be £100;
    (b) if the amount of the financial award is more than £10,000, the amount of the penalty shall be £5,000.
(6) Subsection (7) applies, instead of subsection (5), where an employment tribunal—
    (a) considers together two or more claims involving different workers but the same employer, and
    (b) orders the employer to pay a penalty under this section in respect of any of those claims.
(7) In such a case—
    (a) the amount of the penalties in total shall be at least £100;
    (b) the amount of a penalty in respect of a particular claim shall be—
(i) no more than £5,000, and
(ii) where the tribunal makes a financial award against the employer on the claim, no more than 50% of the amount of the award.
But where the tribunal makes a financial award on any of the claims and the amount awarded is less than £200 in total, the amount of the penalties in total shall be £100 (and paragraphs (a) and (b) shall not apply).
(8) Two or more claims in respect of the same act and the same worker shall be treated as a single claim for the purposes of this section.
(9) Subsection (5) or (7) does not require or permit an order under subsection (1) (or a failure to make such an order) to be reviewed where the tribunal subsequently awards compensation

under—
 (a) section 140. (3) of the Trade Union and Labour Relations (Consolidation) Act 1992 (failure to comply with tribunal's recommendation),
 (b) section 117 of the Employment Rights Act 1996 (failure to reinstate etc.),
 (c) section 124. (7) of the Equality Act 2010 (failure to comply with tribunal's recommendation), or
 (d) any other provision empowering the tribunal to award compensation, or further compensation, for a failure to comply (or to comply fully) with an order or recommendation of the tribunal.
(10) An employer's liability to pay a penalty under this section is discharged if 50% of the amount of the penalty is paid no later than 21 days after the day on which notice of the decision to impose the penalty is sent to the employer.
(11) In this section—
"claim"—
 - means anything that is referred to in the relevant legislation as a claim, a complaint or a reference, other than a reference made by virtue of section 122. (2) or 128. (2) of the Equality Act 2010 (reference by court of question about a non-discrimination or equality rule etc), and
 - also includes an application, under regulations made under section 45 of the Employment Act 2002, for a declaration that a person is a permanent employee;
"employer" has the same meaning as in Part 4. A of the Employment Rights Act 1996, and also—
 - in relation to an individual seeking to be employed by a person as a worker, includes that person;
 - in relation to a right conferred by section 47. A or 63. A of the Employment Rights Act 1996 (right to time off for young person for study or training), includes the principal within the meaning of section 63. A(3) of that Act;
 - in relation to a right conferred by the Agency Workers Regulations 2010 (S.I. 2010/93), includes the hirer within the meaning of those Regulations and (where the worker is not actually employed by the temporary work agency) the temporary work agency within that meaning;
"financial award" means an award of a sum of money, but does not including anything payable by virtue of section 13;
"worker" has the same meaning as in Part 4. A of the Employment Rights Act 1996, and also includes an individual seeking to be employed by a person as a worker.
(12) The Secretary of State may by order—
 (a) amend subsection (3), (5) or (7) by substituting a different amount;
 (b) amend subsection (5), (7) or (10) by substituting a different percentage;
 (c) amend this section so as to alter the meaning of "claim".
[F97. (12. A)Any provision that could be made by an order under subsection (12) may instead—
 (a) in the case of provision that could be made under paragraph (a) or (b) of that subsection, be included in regulations under section 37. N;
 (b) in the case of provision that could be made under paragraph (c) of that subsection, be included in regulations under section 37. Q.]
(13) The Secretary of State shall pay sums received under this section into the Consolidated Fund.]
Amendments (Textual)
F97. S. 12. A(12. A) inserted (6.4.2016) by Small Business, Enterprise and Employment Act 2015 (c. 26), ss. 150. (3), 164. (1) (with s. 150. (8)); S.I. 2016/321, reg. 3. (d)
Modifications etc. (not altering text)
C9. S. 12. A applied (with modifications) by Trade Union and Labour Relations (Consolidation) Act 1992 (c. 52), ss. 138. (2. A), 201. (3. A) as inserted (6.4.2014) by 2013 c. 24, s. 103. (3), Sch. 3 paras. 1, 5 (with s. 24. (5)); S.I. 2014/253, art. 3. (h)

[F98 Costs etc, interest and enforcement]

Amendments (Textual)
F98. S. 13 cross-heading inserted (6.4.2014) by Enterprise and Regulatory Reform Act 2013 (c. 24), s. 103. (3), Sch. 3 para. 3 (with s. 24. (5)); S.I. 2014/253, art. 3. (h)

13 Costs and expenses.

[F99. (1)Employment tribunal procedure regulations may include provision—
  (a) for the award of costs or expenses;
  (b) for the award of any allowances payable under section 5. (2)(c) or (3).
(1. A)Regulations under subsection (1) may include provision authorising an employment tribunal to have regard to a person's ability to pay when considering the making of an award against him under such regulations.
(1. B)Employment tribunal procedure regulations may include provision for authorising an employment tribunal—
  (a) to disallow all or part of the costs or expenses of a representative of a party to proceedings before it by reason of that representative's conduct of the proceedings;
  (b) to order a representative of a party to proceedings before it to meet all or part of the costs or expenses incurred by a party by reason of the representative's conduct of the proceedings;
  (c) to order a representative of a party to proceedings before it to meet all or part of any allowances payable by the Secretary of State under section 5. (2)(c) or (3) by reason of the representative's conduct of the proceedings.
(1. C)Employment tribunal procedure regulations may also include provision for taxing or otherwise settling the costs or expenses referred to in subsection (1)(a) or (1. B)(b) (and, in particular in England and Wales, for enabling the amount of such costs to be assessed by way of detailed assessment in [F100 the county court]).]
(2) In relation to proceedings under section 111 of the M11. Employment Rights Act 1996—
  (a) where the employee has expressed a wish to be reinstated or re-engaged which has been communicated to the employer at least seven days before the hearing of the complaint, F101. . .
    F102. (b). . . . .
[F103employment tribunal] procedure regulations shall include provision for requiring the employer to pay the costs or expenses of any postponement or adjournment of the hearing caused by his failure, without a special reason, to adduce reasonable evidence as to the availability of the job from which the complainant was dismissed F101. . . or of comparable or suitable employment.
[F104. (3)Provision included in employment tribunal procedure regulations under subsection (1) must include provision for requiring an employment tribunal, in any proceedings in which a late postponement application has been granted, to consider whether to make an award against the party who made the application in respect of any costs or expenses connected with the postponement, except in circumstances specified in the regulations.
(4) For the purposes of subsection (3)—
  (a) a late postponement application is an application for the postponement of a hearing in the proceedings which is made after a time determined in accordance with the regulations (whether before or after the hearing has begun), and
  (b) "postponement" includes adjournment.]
Amendments (Textual)
F99. S. 13. (1)-(1. C) substituted (9.7.2004) for s. 13. (1) by 2002 c. 22, ss. 22. (1), 55. (2); S.I. 2004/1717, art. 2. (1)
F100. Words in s. 13. (1. C) substituted (22.4.2014) by Crime and Courts Act 2013 (c. 22), s. 61. (3), Sch. 9 para. 52; S.I. 2014/954, art. 2. (c) (with art. 3) (with transitional provisions and savings in S.I. 2014/956, arts. 3-11)
F101. Words in s. 13. (2)(a)(c) repealed (15.12.1999) by 1999 c. 26, ss. 9, 44, Sch. 4 Pt. III para. 4. (a), Sch. 9. (2); S.I. 1999/2830, art. 2, Sch. 1 Pt. II, Sch. 2 Pt. II

F102. S. 13. (2)(b) repealed (15.12.1999) by 1999 c. 26, ss. 9, 44, Sch. 4 Pt. III para. 4, Sch. 9. (2); S.I. 1999/2830, art. 2, Sch. 1 Pt. II, Sch. 2 Pt. II

F103. Words in s. 13 substituted (1.8.1998) by 1998 c. 8, s. 1. (2)(a) (with s. 16. (2)); S.I. 1998/1658, art. 2. (1), Sch. 1

F104. S. 13. (3)(4) inserted (26.3.2015) by Small Business, Enterprise and Employment Act 2015 (c. 26), ss. 151. (3), 164. (2)(d)

Marginal Citations

M111996 c. 18.

[F10513. A Payments in respect of preparation time

(1) Employment tribunal procedure regulations may include provision for authorising an employment tribunal to order a party to proceedings before it to make a payment to any other party in respect of time spent in preparing that other party's case.

(2) Regulations under subsection (1) may include provision authorising an employment tribunal to have regard to a person's ability to pay when considering the making of an order against him under such regulations.

[F106. (2. A)Provision included in employment tribunal procedure regulations under subsection (1) must include provision for requiring an employment tribunal, in any proceedings in which a late postponement application has been granted, to consider whether to make an order of the kind mentioned in subsection (1) against the party who made the application in respect of any time spent in connection with the postponement, except in circumstances specified in the regulations.

(2. B)For the purposes of subsection (2. A)—

(a) a late postponement application is an application for the postponement of a hearing in the proceedings which is made after a time determined in accordance with the regulations (whether before or after the hearing has begun), and

(b) "postponement" includes adjournment.]

(3) If employment tribunal procedure regulations include—

(a) provision of the kind mentioned in subsection (1), and

(b) provision of the kind mentioned in section 13. (1)(a),

they shall also [F107 , subject to subsection (4),] include provision to prevent an employment tribunal exercising its powers under both kinds of provision in favour of the same person in the same proceedings.]

[F108. (4)Subsection (3) does not require the regulations to include provision to prevent an employment tribunal from making—

(a) an order of the kind mentioned in subsection (1), and

(b) an award of the kind mentioned in section 13. (1)(a) that is limited to witnesses' expenses.]

Amendments (Textual)

F105. S. 13. A inserted (9.7.2004) by 2002 c. 22, ss. 22. (2), 55. (2); S.I. 2004/1717, art. 2. (1)

F106. S. 13. A(2. A)(2. B) inserted (26.3.2015) by Small Business, Enterprise and Employment Act 2015 (c. 26), ss. 151. (4), 164. (2)(d)

F107. Words in s. 13. A(3) inserted (25.6.2013) by Enterprise and Regulatory Reform Act 2013 (c. 24), ss. 21. (3)(a), 103. (2)

F108. S. 13. A(4) inserted (25.4.2013 for specified purposes, 25.6.2016 in so far as not already in force) by Enterprise and Regulatory Reform Act 2013 (c. 24), ss. 21. (3)(b), 103. (1)(i)(2)

14 Interest.

(1) The Secretary of State may by order made with the approval of the Treasury provide that sums payable in pursuance of decisions of [F109employment tribunals] shall carry interest at such rate and between such times as may be prescribed by the order.

(2) Any interest due by virtue of such an order shall be recoverable as a sum payable in pursuance

of the decision.

(3) The power conferred by subsection (1) includes power—

(a) to specify cases or circumstances in which interest is not payable,

(b) to provide that interest is payable only on sums exceeding a specified amount or falling between specified amounts,

(c) to make provision for the manner in which and the periods by reference to which interest is to be calculated and paid,

(d) to provide that any enactment—

(i) does or does not apply in relation to interest payable by virtue of subsection (1), or

(ii) applies to it with such modifications as may be specified in the order,

(e) to make provision for cases where sums are payable in pursuance of decisions or awards made on appeal from [F109employment tribunals],

(f) to make such incidental or supplemental provision as the Secretary of State considers necessary.

(4) In particular, an order under subsection (1) may provide that the rate of interest shall be the rate specified in section 17 of the M12. Judgments Act 1838 as that enactment has effect from time to time.

Amendments (Textual)

F109. Words in s. 14. (1)(3)(e) substituted (1.8.1998) by 1998 c. 8, s. 1. (2)(b) (with s. 16. (2)); S.I. 1998/1658, art. 2. (1), Sch. 1

Marginal Citations

M121838 c. 110.

15 Enforcement.

(1) Any sum payable in pursuance of a decision of an [F110employment tribunal] in England and Wales which has been registered in accordance with [F110employment tribunal] procedure regulations [F111 shall be recoverable [F112 under section 85 of the County Courts Act 1984] or otherwise as if it were payable under an order of [F113 the county court] .]

(2) Any order for the payment of any sum made by an [F110employment tribunal] in Scotland (or any copy of such an order certified by the Secretary of the Tribunals) may be enforced as if it were an extract registered decree arbitral bearing a warrant for execution issued by the sheriff court of any sheriffdom in Scotland.

(3) In this section a reference to a decision or order of an [F110employment tribunal]—

(a) does not include a decision or order which, on being reviewed, has been revoked by the tribunal, and

(b) in relation to a decision or order which on being reviewed, has been varied by the tribunal, shall be construed as a reference to the decision or order as so varied.

Amendments (Textual)

F110. Words in s. 15 substituted (1.8.1998) by 1998 c. 8, s. 1. (2)(a) (with s. 16. (2)); S.I. 1998/1658, art. 2. (1), Sch. 1

F111. Words in s. 15. (1) substituted (1.4.2009) by Tribunals, Courts and Enforcement Act 2007 (c. 15), s. 148, Sch. 8 para. 43; S.I. 2008/2696, art. 6. (b)(ii)

F112. Words in s. 15. (1) substituted (6.4.2014) by Tribunals, Courts and Enforcement Act 2007 (c. 15), s. 148, Sch. 13 para. 125 (with s. 89); S.I. 2014/768, art. 2. (1)(b)

F113. Words in s. 15. (1) substituted (22.4.2014) by Crime and Courts Act 2013 (c. 22), s. 61. (3), Sch. 9 para. 52; S.I. 2014/954, art. 2. (c) (with art. 3) (with transitional provisions and savings in S.I. 2014/956, arts. 3-11)

Recoupment of social security benefits

16 Power to provide for recoupment of benefits.

(1) This section applies to payments which are the subject of proceedings before [F114employment tribunals] and which are—

(a) payments of wages or compensation for loss of wages,

(b) payments by employers to employees under sections 146 to 151, sections 168 to 173 or section 192 of the M13. Trade Union and Labour Relations (Consolidation) Act 1992,

(c) payments by employers to employees under—

(i) Part III, V, VI or VII,

(ii) section 93, or

(iii) Part X,

of the M14. Employment Rights Act 1996, F115...

(d) payments by employers to employees of a nature similar to, or for a purpose corresponding to the purpose of, payments within paragraph (b) or (c),[F116or

(e) payments by employers to employees under regulation 5, 6 or 9 of the Employment Relations Act 1999 (Blacklists) Regulations 2010,]

and to payments of remuneration under a protective award under section 189 of the Trade Union and Labour Relations (Consolidation) Act 1992.

(2) The Secretary of State may by regulations make with respect to payments to which this section applies provision for any or all of the purposes specified in subsection (3).

(3) The purposes referred to in subsection (2) are—

(a) enabling the Secretary of State to recover from an employer, by way of total or partial recoupment of [F117universal credit,] jobseeker's allowance [F118 , income support or income-related employment and support allowance] —

(i) a sum not exceeding the amount of the prescribed element of the monetary award, or

(ii) in the case of a protective award, the amount of the remuneration,

(b) requiring or authorising an [F114employment tribunal] to order the payment of such a sum, by way of total or partial recoupment of [F119universal credit,] [F120jobseeker's allowance, income support or income-related employment and support allowance] , to the Secretary of State instead of to an employee, and

(c) requiring an [F114employment tribunal] to order the payment to an employee of only the excess of the prescribed element of the monetary award over the amount of any [F121universal credit,] jobseeker's allowance [F122 , income support or income-related employment and support allowance] shown to the tribunal to have been paid to the employee and enabling the Secretary of State to recover from the employer, by way of total or partial recoupment of the benefit, a sum not exceeding that amount.

(4) Regulations under this section may be framed—

(a) so as to apply to all payments to which this section applies or to one or more classes of those payments, and

[F123. (b)so as to apply to all or any of the benefits mentioned in subsection (3).]

(5) Regulations under this section may—

(a) confer powers and impose duties on [F114employment tribunals] or [F124adjudication officers or] other persons,

(b) impose on an employer to whom a monetary award or protective award relates a duty—

(i) to furnish particulars connected with the award, and

(ii) to suspend payments in pursuance of the award during any period prescribed by the regulations,

(c) provide for an employer who pays a sum to the Secretary of State in pursuance of this section to be relieved from any liability to pay the sum to another person,

[F125. (cc)provide for the determination by the Secretary of State of any issue arising as to the total or partial recoupment in pursuance of the regulations of [F126universal credit,] a jobseeker's allowance, unemployment benefit [F127 , income support or income-related employment and support allowance],

F125. (d)confer on an employee a right of appeal to [F128the First-tier Tribunal] against any decision of the Secretary of State on any such issue, and]

(e) provide for the proof in proceedings before [F114employment tribunals] (whether by certificate or in any other manner) of any amount of [F129universal credit,] jobseeker's allowance [F130 , income support or income-related employment and support allowance] paid to an employee.

(6) Regulations under this section may make different provision for different cases.

Amendments (Textual)

F114. Words in s. 16. (1)(3)(c)(5)(a)(e) substituted (1.8.1998) by 1998 c. 8, s. 1. (2)(a)(b) (with s. 16. (2)); S.I. 1998/1658, art. 2. (1), Sch. 1

F115. Word in s. 16. (1)(c) omitted (2.3.2010) by virtue of The Employment Relations Act 1999 (Blacklists) Regulations 2010 (S.I. 2010/493), regs. 1. (b), 17. (3)(a)

F116. S. 16. (1)(e) and word inserted (2.3.2010) by The Employment Relations Act 1999 (Blacklists) Regulations 2010 (S.I. 2010/493), regs. 1. (b), 17. (3)(b)

F117. Words in s. 16. (3)(a) inserted (29.4.2013) by The Universal Credit (Consequential, Supplementary, Incidental and Miscellaneous Provisions) Regulations 2013 (S.I. 2013/630), regs. 1. (2), 11. (2)(a)

F118. Words in s. 16. (3)(a) substituted (18.3.2008 for specified purposes, 27.10.2008 in so far as not already in force) by Welfare Reform Act 2007 (c. 5), s. 70. (2), Sch. 3 para. 15. (2)(a); S.I. 2008/787, art. 2. (1)(4)(f), Sch.

F119. Words in s. 16. (3)(b) inserted (29.4.2013) by The Universal Credit (Consequential, Supplementary, Incidental and Miscellaneous Provisions) Regulations 2013 (S.I. 2013/630), regs. 1. (2), 11. (2)(a)

F120. Words in s. 16. (3)(b) substituted (18.3.2008 for specified purposes, 27.10.2008 in so far as not already in force) by Welfare Reform Act 2007 (c. 5), s. 70. (2), Sch. 3 para. 15. (2)(b); S.I. 2008/787, art. 2. (1)(4)(f), Sch.

F121. Words in s. 16. (3)(c) inserted (29.4.2013) by The Universal Credit (Consequential, Supplementary, Incidental and Miscellaneous Provisions) Regulations 2013 (S.I. 2013/630), regs. 1. (2), 11. (2)(a)

F122. Words in s. 16. (3)(c) substituted (18.3.2008 for specified purposes, 27.10.2008 in so far as not already in force) by Welfare Reform Act 2007 (c. 5), s. 70. (2), Sch. 3 para. 15. (2)(a); S.I. 2008/787, art. 2. (1)(4)(f), Sch.

F123. S. 16. (4)(b) substituted (18.3.2008 for specified purposes, 27.10.2008 in so far as not already in force) by Welfare Reform Act 2007 (c. 5), s. 70. (2), Sch. 3 para. 15. (2)(c); S.I. 2008/787, art. 2. (1)(4)(f), Sch.

F124. Words in s. 16. (5)(a) repealed (18.10.1999 and 29.11.1999 for certain purposes and otherwise prosp.) by 1998 c. 14, s. 86. (1)(2), Sch. 7 para. 147. (a), Sch. 8; S.I. 1999/2860, art. 2 (subject to transitional provisions in Schs. 16-18); S.I. 1999/3178, art. 2. (1), Sch. 1 (subject to transitional provisions in Schs. 21-23)

F125. S. 16. (5)(cc)(d) substituted for s. 16. (5)(d) (18.10.1999 and 29.11.1999 for certain purposes and otherwise prosp.) by 1998 c. 14, s. 86. (1), Sch. 7 para. 147. (b); S.I. 1999/2860, art. 2 (subject to transitional provisions in Schs. 16-18); S.I. 1999/3178, art. 2. (1), Sch. 1 (subject to transitional provisions in Schs. 21-23)

F126. Words in s. 16. (5)(cc) inserted (29.4.2013) by The Universal Credit (Consequential, Supplementary, Incidental and Miscellaneous Provisions) Regulations 2013 (S.I. 2013/630), regs. 1. (2), 11. (3)

F127. Words in s. 16. (5)(cc) substituted (18.3.2008 for specified purposes, 27.10.2008 in so far as not already in force) by Welfare Reform Act 2007 (c. 5), s. 70. (2), Sch. 3 para. 15. (2)(a); S.I. 2008/787, art. 2. (1)(4)(f), Sch.

F128. Words in s. 16. (5)(d) substituted (3.11.2008) by The Transfer of Tribunal Functions Order 2008 (S.I. 2008/2833), art. 1. (1), Sch. 3 para. 137

F129. Words in s. 16. (5)(e) inserted (29.4.2013) by The Universal Credit (Consequential,

Supplementary, Incidental and Miscellaneous Provisions) Regulations 2013 (S.I. 2013/630), regs. 1. (2), 11. (2)(b)

F130. Words in s. 16. (5)(e) substituted (18.3.2008 for specified purposes, 27.10.2008 in so far as not already in force) by Welfare Reform Act 2007 (c. 5), s. 70. (2), Sch. 3 para. 15. (2)(a); S.I. 2008/787, art. 2. (1)(4)(f), Sch.

Marginal Citations
M131992 c. 52.
M141996 c. 18.

17 Recoupment: further provisions.

(1) Where in pursuance of any regulations under section 16 a sum has been recovered by or paid to the Secretary of State by way of total or partial recoupment of [F131universal credit,] jobseeker's allowance [F132 , income support or income-related employment and support allowance] —

(a) no sum shall be recoverable under Part III or V of the M15. Social Security Administration Act 1992, and

(b) no abatement, payment or reduction shall be made by reference to the [F133universal credit,] jobseeker's allowance [F132 , income support or income-related employment and support allowance] recouped.

(2) Any amount found to have been duly recovered by or paid to the Secretary of State in pursuance of regulations under section 16 by way of total or partial recoupment of jobseeker's allowance shall be paid into the National Insurance Fund.

(3) In section 16—

"monetary award" means the amount which is awarded, or ordered to be paid, to the employee by the tribunal or would be so awarded or ordered apart from any provision of regulations under that section, and

"the prescribed element", in relation to any monetary award, means so much of that award as is attributable to such matters as may be prescribed by regulations under that section.

(4) In section 16 "income-based jobseeker's allowance" has the same meaning as in the M16. Jobseekers Act 1995.

[F134. (5)In this section and section 16 "income-related employment and support allowance" means an income-related allowance under Part 1 of the Welfare Reform Act 2007 (employment and support allowance).]

Amendments (Textual)

F131. Words in s. 17. (1) inserted (29.4.2013) by The Universal Credit (Consequential, Supplementary, Incidental and Miscellaneous Provisions) Regulations 2013 (S.I. 2013/630), regs. 1. (2), 11. (4)

F132. Words in s. 17. (1) substituted (18.3.2008 for specified purposes, 27.10.2008 in so far as not already in force) by Welfare Reform Act 2007 (c. 5), s. 70. (2), Sch. 3 para. 15. (3); S.I. 2008/787, art. 2. (1)(4)(f), Sch.

F133. Words in s. 17. (1)(b) inserted (29.4.2013) by The Universal Credit (Consequential, Supplementary, Incidental and Miscellaneous Provisions) Regulations 2013 (S.I. 2013/630), regs. 1. (2), 11. (4)

F134. S. 17. (5) inserted (18.3.2008 for specified purposes, 27.10.2008 in so far as not already in force) by Welfare Reform Act 2007 (c. 5), s. 70. (2), Sch. 3 para. 15. (4); S.I. 2008/787, art. 2. (1)(4)(f), Sch.

Marginal Citations
M151992 c. 5.
M161995 c. 18.

Conciliation

18 Conciliation [F135: relevant proceedings etc.].

[F136. (1) In this section and sections 18. A to 18. C "relevant proceedings" means employment tribunal proceedings—]
[F137. (a) under section 66, 68. A, 70. C, 87, 137, 138, 145. A, 145. B, 146, 168, 168. A, 169, 170, 174, 189 or 192 of, or paragraph 156 of Schedule A1 to, the Trade Union and Labour Relations (Consolidation) Act 1992,
(b) under section 11, 23, 34, 63. I, 70, 70. A, 80. (1), 80. H, 93, 111, 163 or 177 of the Employment Rights Act 1996, or under Part 5 or 6 of that Act,
(c) under section 11, 19. D(1)(a) or 24 of the National Minimum Wage Act 1998,
(d) under section 56 of the Pensions Act 2008,
(e) under section 120 or 127 of the Equality Act 2010,
(f) under regulation 11 of the Safety Representatives and Safety Committees Regulations 1977,
(g) under article 6 of the Employment Tribunals Extension of Jurisdiction (England and Wales) Order 1994,
(h) under article 6 of the Employment Tribunals Extension of Jurisdiction (Scotland) Order 1994,
(i) under paragraph 2 of Schedule 2 to the Health and Safety (Consultation with Employees) Regulations 1996,
(j) under regulation 30 of the Working Time Regulations 1998,
(k) under regulation 27 or 32 of the Transnational Information and Consultation of Employees Regulation 1999,
(l) under regulation 8 of the Part-time Workers (Prevention of Less Favourable Treatment) Regulations 2000,
(m) under regulation 7 or 9 of the Fixed-term Employees (Prevention of Less Favourable Treatment) Regulations 2002,
(n) under regulation 22 of the Merchant Shipping (Hours of Work) Regulations 2002,
(o) under regulation 15 of the Flexible Working (Procedural Requirements) Regulations 2002,
(p) under regulation 18 of the Merchant Shipping (Working Time: Inland Waterways) Regulations 2003,
(q) under regulation 18 of the Civil Aviation (Working Time) Regulations 2004,
(r) under regulation 19 of the Fishing Vessels (Working Time: Sea-fishermen) Regulations 2004,
(s) under regulation 29 or 33 of the Information and Consultation of Employees Regulations 2004,
(t) under paragraphs 4 or 8 of the Schedule to the Occupational and Personal Pension Schemes (Consultation by Employers and Miscellaneous Amendment) Regulations 2006,
(u) under regulation 30 or 34 of the European Cooperative Society (Involvement of Employees) Regulations 2006,
(v) under regulation 45 or 51 of the Companies (Cross-Border Mergers) Regulations 2007,
(w) under regulation 17 of the Cross-border Railway Services (Working Time) Regulations 2008,
(x) under regulation 9 of Ecclesiastical Offices (Terms of Service) Regulations 2009,
(y) under regulation 28 or 32 of the European Public Limited-Liability Company (Employee Involvement) (Great Britain) Regulations 2009,
(z) under regulation 18 of the Agency Workers Regulations 2010,
(z1) under regulation 17 of the Employee Study and Training (Procedural Requirements) Regulations 2010, F138...
(z2) under regulation 5, 6 or 9 of the Employment Relations Act 1999 (Blacklists) Regulations 2010.] [F139, F140...
(z3) under regulation 3 of the Exclusivity Terms in Zero Hours Contracts (Redress) Regulations

2015.][F141, or

(z4) under regulation 6 of the Posted Workers (Enforcement of Employment Rights) Regulations 2016.]

[F142. (1. A)Sections 18. A and 18. B apply in the case of matters which could be the subject of relevant proceedings, and section 18. C applies in the case of relevant proceedings themselves.]

F143. (2)................................

[F144. (2. A)F145...............................]

F143. (3)................................

F143. (4)................................

F143. (5)................................

(6) In proceeding under [F146any of sections 18. A to 18. C] a conciliation officer shall, where appropriate, have regard to the desirability of encouraging the use of other procedures available for the settlement of grievances.

(7) Anything communicated to a conciliation officer in connection with the performance of his functions under [F146any of sections 18. A to 18. C] shall not be admissible in evidence in any proceedings before an [F147employment tribunal], except with the consent of the person who communicated it to that officer.

(8) The Secretary of State [F148and the Lord Chancellor, acting jointly,] may by order [F149amend the definition of "relevant proceedings" in subsection (1) by adding to or removing from the list in that subsection particular types of employment tribunal proceedings.]

[F150. (9)An order under subsection (8) that adds employment tribunal proceedings to the list in subsection (1) may amend an enactment so as to extend the time limit for instituting those proceedings in such a way as appears necessary or expedient in order to facilitate the conciliation process provided for by section 18. A.

(10) An order under subsection (8) that removes employment tribunal proceedings from the list in subsection (1) may—

(a) repeal or revoke any provision of an enactment that, for the purpose mentioned in subsection (9), extends the time limit for instituting those proceedings;

(b) make further amendments which are consequential on that repeal or revocation.]

Amendments (Textual)

F135. Words in s. 18 heading inserted (6.4.2014) by Enterprise and Regulatory Reform Act 2013 (c. 24), s. 103. (3), Sch. 1 para. 5. (2); S.I. 2014/253, art. 3. (f)

F136. Words in s. 18. (1) substituted (6.4.2014) by Enterprise and Regulatory Reform Act 2013 (c. 24), s. 103. (3), Sch. 1 para. 5. (3); S.I. 2014/253, art. 3. (f)

F137. S. 18. (1)(a)-(z2) substituted for s. 18. (1)(a)-(y) (6.4.2014) by The Employment Tribunals Act 1996 (Application of Conciliation Provisions) Order 2014 (S.I. 2014/431), arts. 1, 2

F138. Word in s. 18. (1) omitted (11.1.2016) by virtue of The Employment Tribunals Act 1996 (Application of Conciliation Provisions) Order 2015 (S.I. 2015/2054), arts. 1, 2. (2)(a)

F139. S. 18. (1)(z3) and word inserted (11.1.2016) by The Employment Tribunals Act 1996 (Application of Conciliation Provisions) Order 2015 (S.I. 2015/2054), arts. 1, 2. (2)(b)

F140. Word in s. 18. (1) omitted (18.6.2016) by virtue of The Posted Workers (Enforcement of Employment Rights) Regulations 2016 (S.I. 2016/539), regs. 1. (1), 10. (2)(a)

F141. S. 18. (1)(z4) and word inserted (18.6.2016) by The Posted Workers (Enforcement of Employment Rights) Regulations 2016 (S.I. 2016/539), regs. 1. (1), 10. (2)(b)

F142. S. 18. (1. A) inserted (6.4.2014) by Enterprise and Regulatory Reform Act 2013 (c. 24), s. 103. (3), Sch. 1 para. 5. (7); S.I. 2014/253, art. 3. (f)

F143. S. 18. (2)-(5) omitted (6.4.2014) by virtue of Enterprise and Regulatory Reform Act 2013 (c. 24), s. 103. (3), Sch. 1 para. 5. (8); S.I. 2014/253, art. 3. (f) (with art. 5. (2))

F144. S. 18. (2. A) inserted (9.7.2004) by 2002 c. 22, ss. 24. (2), 55. (2); S.I. 2004/1717, art. 2. (1)

F145. S. 18. (2. A) repealed (6.4.2009) by Employment Act 2008 (c. 24), ss. 6. (1), 22. (1)(a), Sch. Pt. 1; S.I. 2008/3232, art. 2 (with art. 3, Sch.)

F146. Words in s. 18. (6)(7) substituted (6.4.2014) by Enterprise and Regulatory Reform Act 2013 (c. 24), s. 103. (3), Sch. 1 para. 5. (9); S.I. 2014/253, art. 3. (f) (with art. 5. (1))

F147. Words in s. 18 substituted (1.8.1998) by 1998 c. 8, s. 1. (2)(a) (with s. 16. (2)); S.I. 1998/1658, art. 2. (1), Sch. 1

F148. Words in s. 18. (8) inserted (1.12.2007) by Tribunals, Courts and Enforcement Act 2007 (c. 15), ss. 48. (1), 148, Sch. 8 para. 38; S.I. 2007/2709, art. 4

F149. Words in s 18. (8) substituted for s. 18. (8)(a)(b) (25.4.2013 for specified purposes, 6.4.2014 in so far as not already in force) by Enterprise and Regulatory Reform Act 2013 (c. 24), ss. 9. (2), 103. (1)(i)(3); S.I. 2014/253, art. 3. (d)

F150. S. 18. (9)(10) inserted (25.4.2013 for specified purposes, 6.4.2014 in so far as not already in force) by Enterprise and Regulatory Reform Act 2013 (c. 24), ss. 9. (3), 103. (1)(i)(3); S.I. 2014/253, art. 3. (d)

Modifications etc. (not altering text)

C10. S. 18 applied (6.4.2006 with application as mentioned in reg. 21. (1) of the applying S.I.) by The Transfer of Undertakings (Protection of Employment) Regulations 2006 (S.I. 2006/246), reg. 16. (1) (with reg. 21. (5))

S. 18 applied (6.4.2006 with application as mentioned in reg. 21. (1) of the applying S.I.) by The Transfer of Undertakings (Protection of Employment) Regulations 2006 (S.I. 2006/246), reg. 12. (7)

[F15118. ARequirement to contact ACAS before instituting proceedings

(1) Before a person ("the prospective claimant") presents an application to institute relevant proceedings relating to any matter, the prospective claimant must provide to ACAS prescribed information, in the prescribed manner, about that matter.
This is subject to subsection (7).
(2) On receiving the prescribed information in the prescribed manner, ACAS shall send a copy of it to a conciliation officer.
(3) The conciliation officer shall, during the prescribed period, endeavour to promote a settlement between the persons who would be parties to the proceedings.
(4) If—
    (a) during the prescribed period the conciliation officer concludes that a settlement is not possible, or
    (b) the prescribed period expires without a settlement having been reached,
the conciliation officer shall issue a certificate to that effect, in the prescribed manner, to the prospective claimant.
(5) The conciliation officer may continue to endeavour to promote a settlement after the expiry of the prescribed period.
(6) In subsections (3) to (5) "settlement" means a settlement that avoids proceedings being instituted.
(7) A person may institute relevant proceedings without complying with the requirement in subsection (1) in prescribed cases.
The cases that may be prescribed include (in particular)—
cases where the requirement is complied with by another person instituting relevant proceedings relating to the same matter;
cases where proceedings that are not relevant proceedings are instituted by means of the same form as proceedings that are;
cases where section 18. B applies because ACAS has been contacted by a person against whom relevant proceedings are being instituted.
(8) A person who is subject to the requirement in subsection (1) may not present an application to institute relevant proceedings without a certificate under subsection (4).
(9) Where a conciliation officer acts under this section in a case where the prospective claimant has ceased to be employed by the employer and the proposed proceedings are proceedings under

section 111 of the Employment Rights Act 1996, the conciliation officer may in particular—

(a) seek to promote the reinstatement or re-engagement of the prospective claimant by the employer, or by a successor of the employer or by an associated employer, on terms appearing to the conciliation officer to be equitable, or

(b) where the prospective claimant does not wish to be reinstated or re-engaged, or where reinstatement or re-engagement is not practicable, seek to promote agreement between them as to a sum by way of compensation to be paid by the employer to the prospective claimant.

(10) In subsections (1) to (7) "prescribed" means prescribed in employment tribunal procedure regulations.

(11) The Secretary of State may by employment tribunal procedure regulations make such further provision as appears to the Secretary of State to be necessary or expedient with respect to the conciliation process provided for by subsections (1) to (8).

(12) Employment tribunal procedure regulations may (in particular) make provision—

(a) authorising the Secretary of State to prescribe, or prescribe requirements in relation to, any form which is required by such regulations to be used for the purpose of providing information to ACAS under subsection (1) or issuing a certificate under subsection (4);

(b) requiring ACAS to give a person any necessary assistance to comply with the requirement in subsection (1);

(c) for the extension of the period prescribed for the purposes of subsection (3);

(d) treating the requirement in subsection (1) as complied with, for the purposes of any provision extending the time limit for instituting relevant proceedings, by a person who is relieved of that requirement by virtue of subsection (7)(a).

Amendments (Textual)

F151. Ss. 18. A, 18. B inserted (25.4.2013 for specified purposes, 6.4.2014 in so far as not already in force) by Enterprise and Regulatory Reform Act 2013 (c. 24), ss. 7. (1), 103. (1)(i)(3); S.I. 2014/253, art. 3. (a)(b) (with arts. 4, 5)

18. BConciliation before institution of proceedings: other ACAS duties

(1) This section applies where—

(a) a person contacts ACAS requesting the services of a conciliation officer in relation to a matter that (if not settled) is likely to give rise to relevant proceedings against that person, and

(b) ACAS has not received information from the prospective claimant under section 18. A(1).

(2) This section also applies where—

(a) a person contacts ACAS requesting the services of a conciliation officer in relation to a matter that (if not settled) is likely to give rise to relevant proceedings by that person, and

(b) the requirement in section 18. A(1) would apply to that person but for section 18. A(7).

(3) Where this section applies a conciliation officer shall endeavour to promote a settlement between the persons who would be parties to the proceedings.

(4) If at any time—

(a) the conciliation officer concludes that a settlement is not possible, or

(b) a conciliation officer comes under the duty in section 18. A(3) to promote a settlement between the persons who would be parties to the proceedings,

the duty in subsection (3) ceases to apply at that time.

(5) In subsections (3) and (4) "settlement" means a settlement that avoids proceedings being instituted.

(6) Subsection (9) of section 18. A applies for the purposes of this section as it applies for the purposes of that section.]

Amendments (Textual)

F151. Ss. 18. A, 18. B inserted (25.4.2013 for specified purposes, 6.4.2014 in so far as not already in force) by Enterprise and Regulatory Reform Act 2013 (c. 24), ss. 7. (1), 103. (1)(i)(3); S.I.

2014/253, art. 3. (a)(b) (with arts. 4, 5)

[F15218. CConciliation after institution of proceedings

(1) Where an application instituting relevant proceedings has been presented to an employment tribunal, and a copy of it has been sent to a conciliation officer, the conciliation officer shall endeavour to promote a settlement—
　(a) if requested to do so by the person by whom and the person against whom the proceedings are brought, or
　(b) if, in the absence of any such request, the conciliation officer considers that the officer could act under this section with a reasonable prospect of success.
(2) Where a person who has presented a complaint to an employment tribunal under section 111 of the Employment Rights Act 1996 has ceased to be employed by the employer against whom the complaint was made, the conciliation officer may in particular—
　(a) seek to promote the reinstatement or re-engagement of the complainant by the employer, or by a successor of the employer or by an associated employer, on terms appearing to the conciliation officer to be equitable, or
　(b) where the complainant does not wish to be reinstated or re-engaged, or where reinstatement or re-engagement is not practicable, and the parties desire the conciliation officer to act, seek to promote agreement between them as to a sum by way of compensation to be paid by the employer to the complainant.
(3) In subsection (1) "settlement" means a settlement that brings proceedings to an end without their being determined by an employment tribunal.]
Amendments (Textual)
F152. S. 18. C inserted (6.4.2014) by Enterprise and Regulatory Reform Act 2013 (c. 24), s. 103. (3), Sch. 1 para. 6; S.I. 2014/253, art. 3. (f)

19 Conciliation procedure.

[F153. (1)][F154. Employment tribunal] procedure regulations shall include in relation to [F154employment tribunal] proceedings in the case of which any enactment makes provision for conciliation—
　(a) provisions requiring a copy of the application by which the proceedings are instituted, and a copy of any notice relating to it which is lodged by or on behalf of the person against whom the proceedings are brought, to be sent to a conciliation officer, [F155and]
　(b) provisions securing that the applicant and the person against whom the proceedings are brought are notified that the services of a conciliation officer are available to them, F156. . .
　　F156. (c). . . . .
[F157. (2)F158. . . . .]
Amendments (Textual)
F153. S. 19 renumbered (9.7.2004) as s. 19. (1) by 2002 c. 22, ss. 24. (4), 55. (2); S.I. 2004/1717, art. 2. (1)
F154. Words in s. 19 substituted (1.8.1998) by 1998 c. 8, s. 1. (2)(a) (with s. 16. (2)); S.I. 1998/1658, art. 2. (1), Sch. 1
F155. Word in s. 19. (a) inserted (1.10.2004) by Employment Act 2002 (c. 22), ss. 53, 55. (2), Sch. 7 para. 23. (3); S.I. 2004/2185, art. 2
F156. S. 19. (c) and word immediately before it repealed (6.4.2003) by 2002 c. 22, ss. 24. (3), 54, Sch. 8; S.I. 2002/2866, art. 2. (4)(5), Sch. 2 Pt. 2
F157. S. 19. (2) inserted (9.7.2004) by 2002 c. 22, ss. 24. (4), 55. (2); S.I. 2004/1717, art. 2. (1)
F158. S. 19. (2) repealed (6.4.2009) by Employment Act 2008 (c. 24), ss. 6. (2), 22. (1)(a), Sch. Pt. 1; S.I. 2008/3232, art. 2 (with art. 3, Sch.)

[F15919. AConciliation: recovery of sums payable under [F160 settlements]

(1) Subsections (3) to (6) apply if—
   (a) a conciliation officer—
(i) has taken action under [F161 any of sections 18. A to 18. C] in a case, and
(ii) issues a certificate in writing stating that a [F162 settlement] has been reached in the case, and
   (b) all of the terms of the [F162 settlement] are set out—
(i) in a single relevant document, or
(ii) in a combination of two or more relevant documents.
(2) A document is a "relevant document" for the purposes of subsection (1) if—
   (a) it is the certificate, or
   (b) it is a document that is referred to in the certificate or that is referred to in a document that is within this paragraph.
(3) Any sum payable by a person under the terms of the [F163 settlement] (a " [F163 settlement] sum"), shall, subject to subsections (4) to (7), be recoverable—
   (a) in England and Wales, by execution issued from [F164 the county court] or otherwise as if the sum were payable under an order of that court;
   (b) in Scotland, by diligence as if the certificate were an extract registered decree arbitral bearing a warrant for execution issued by the sheriff court of any sheriffdom in Scotland.
(4) A [F165 settlement] sum is not recoverable under subsection (3) if—
   (a) the person by whom it is payable applies for a declaration that the sum would not be recoverable from him under the general law of contract, and
   (b) that declaration is made.
(5) If rules of court so provide, a [F166 settlement] sum is not recoverable under subsection (3) during the period—
   (a) beginning with the issue of the certificate, and
   (b) ending at such time as may be specified in, or determined under, rules of court.
(6) If the terms of the [F167 settlement] provide for the person to whom a [F167 settlement] sum is payable to do anything in addition to discontinuing or not starting proceedings, that sum is recoverable by him under subsection (3)—
   (a) in England and Wales, only if [F164 the county court] so orders;
   (b) in Scotland, only if the sheriff so orders.
(7) Once an application has been made for a declaration under subsection (4) in relation to a sum, no further reliance may be placed on subsection (3) for the recovery of the sum while the application is pending.
(8) An application for a declaration under subsection (4) may be made to an employment tribunal, [F164 the county court] or the sheriff.
(9) Employment tribunal procedure regulations may (in particular) make provision as to the time within which an application to an employment tribunal for a declaration under subsection (4) is to be made.
(10) Rules of court may make provision as to—
   (a) the time within which an application to [F164 the county court] for a declaration under subsection (4) is to be made;
   (b) the time within which an application to the sheriff for a declaration under subsection (4) is to be made;
   (c) when an application (whether made to [F164 the county court] , the sheriff or an employment tribunal) for a declaration under subsection (4) is pending for the purposes of subsection (7).
[F168. (10. A)A term of any document which is a relevant document for the purposes of subsection (1) is void to the extent that it purports to prevent the disclosure of any provision of any such document to a person appointed or authorised to act under section 37. M.]

(11) Nothing in this section shall be taken to prejudice any rights or remedies that a person has apart from this section.
(12) In this section " [F169 settlement] " (except in the phrase " [F169 settlement] sum") means a settlementF170... to avoid proceedings or bring proceedings to an end.]
Amendments (Textual)
F159. S. 19. A inserted (1.4.2009) by Tribunals, Courts and Enforcement Act 2007 (c. 15), ss. 142, 148; S.I. 2008/2696, art. 6. (a)
F160. Word in s. 19. A heading substituted (29.7.2013) by Enterprise and Regulatory Reform Act 2013 (c. 24), ss. 23. (2)(c), 103. (3); S.I. 2013/1648, art. 2. (c)
F161. Words in s. 19. A(1)(a)(i) substituted (6.4.2014) by Enterprise and Regulatory Reform Act 2013 (c. 24), s. 103. (3), Sch. 1 para. 7; S.I. 2014/253, art. 3. (f) (with art. 5. (1))
F162. Word in s. 19. A(1) substituted (29.7.2013) by Enterprise and Regulatory Reform Act 2013 (c. 24), ss. 23. (2)(a), 103. (3); S.I. 2013/1648, art. 2. (c)
F163. Word in s. 19. A(3) substituted (29.7.2013) by Enterprise and Regulatory Reform Act 2013 (c. 24), ss. 23. (2)(a), 103. (3); S.I. 2013/1648, art. 2. (c)
F164. Words in s. 19. A substituted (22.4.2014) by Crime and Courts Act 2013 (c. 22), s. 61. (3), Sch. 9 para. 52; S.I. 2014/954, art. 2. (c) (with art. 3) (with transitional provisions and savings in S.I. 2014/956, arts. 3-11)
F165. Word in s. 19. A(4) substituted (29.7.2013) by Enterprise and Regulatory Reform Act 2013 (c. 24), ss. 23. (2)(a), 103. (3); S.I. 2013/1648, art. 2. (c)
F166. Word in s. 19. A(5) substituted (29.7.2013) by Enterprise and Regulatory Reform Act 2013 (c. 24), ss. 23. (2)(a), 103. (3); S.I. 2013/1648, art. 2. (c)
F167. Word in s. 19. A(6) substituted (29.7.2013) by Enterprise and Regulatory Reform Act 2013 (c. 24), ss. 23. (2)(a), 103. (3); S.I. 2013/1648, art. 2. (c)
F168. S. 19. A(10. A) inserted (6.4.2016) by Small Business, Enterprise and Employment Act 2015 (c. 26), ss. 150. (4), 164. (1) (with s. 150. (8)); S.I. 2016/321, reg. 3. (d)
F169. Word in s. 19. A(12) substituted (29.7.2013) by Enterprise and Regulatory Reform Act 2013 (c. 24), ss. 23. (2)(b)(i), 103. (3); S.I. 2013/1648, art. 2. (c)
F170. Words in s. 19. A(12) omitted (29.7.2013) by virtue of Enterprise and Regulatory Reform Act 2013 (c. 24), ss. 23. (2)(b)(ii), 103. (3); S.I. 2013/1648, art. 2. (c)

Part II The Employment Appeal Tribunal

Part II The Employment Appeal Tribunal

20 The Appeal Tribunal.

(1) The Employment Appeal Tribunal ("the Appeal Tribunal") shall continue in existence.
(2) The Appeal Tribunal shall have a central office in London but may sit at any time and in any place in Great Britain.
(3) The Appeal Tribunal shall be a superior court of record and shall have an official seal which shall be judicially noticed.
[F1. (4)Subsection (2) is subject to regulation 34 of the Transnational Information and Consultation of Employees Regulations [F21999,] [F3 regulation 46. (1) of the European Public Limited-Liability Company Regulations [F42004,]] [F5 regulation 36. (1) of the Information and Consultation of Employees Regulations [F62004,]] [F7regulation 37. (1) of the European Cooperative Society (Involvement of Employees) Regulations [F82006,]] [F9regulation 58. (1) of the Companies (Cross-Border Mergers) Regulations 2007] [F10and regulation 33. (1) of the European Public Limited-Liability Company (Employee Involvement) (Great Britain) Regulations

2009. (S.I. 2009/2401)].]
Amendments (Textual)
F1. S. 20. (4) inserted (15.1.2000) by S.I. 1999/3323, reg. 35. (2)
F2. Words in s. 20. (4) substituted (6. 4 2005) by The Information and Consultation of Employees Regulations 2004 (S.I. 2004/3426), reg. 36. (2)(a) (with reg. 3)
F3. Words in s. 20. (4) inserted (8.10.2004) by The European Public Limited-Liability Company Regulations 2004 (S.I. 2004/2326), reg. 48. (2)
F4. Words in s. 20. (4) substituted (18.8.2006) by The European Cooperative Society (Involvement of Employees) Regulations 2006 (S.I. 2006/2059), reg. 37. (2)(a)
F5. Words in s. 20. (4) inserted (6. 4 2005) by The Information and Consultation of Employees Regulations 2004 (S.I. 2004/3426), reg. 36. (2)(b) (with reg. 3)
F6. Words in s. 20. (4) substituted (15.12.2007) by The Companies (Cross-Border Mergers) Regulations 2007 (S.I. 2007/2974), reg. 58. (2)(a)
F7. Words in s. 20. (4) substituted (18.8.2006) by The European Cooperative Society (Involvement of Employees) Regulations 2006 (S.I. 2006/2059), reg. 37. (2)(b)
F8. Words in s. 20. (4) substituted (1.10.2009) by The European Public Limited-Liability Company (Employee Involvement) (Great Britain) Regulations 2009 (S.I. 2009/2401), regs. 1. (2), 35. (2)(a) (with regs. 4, 41)
F9. Words in s. 20. (4) substituted (15.12.2007) by The Companies (Cross-Border Mergers) Regulations 2007 (S.I. 2007/2974), reg. 58. (2)(b)
F10. Words in s. 20. (4) inserted (1.10.2009) by The European Public Limited-Liability Company (Employee Involvement) (Great Britain) Regulations 2009 (S.I. 2009/2401), regs. 1. (2), 35. (2)(b) (with regs. 4, 41)

Jurisdiction

21 Jurisdiction of Appeal Tribunal.

(1) An appeal lies to the Appeal Tribunal on any question of law arising from any decision of, or arising in any proceedings before, an [F11employment tribunal] under or by virtue of—
    F12. (a)...............................
    F12. (b)...............................
    F12. (c)...............................
    (d) M1 the Trade Union and Labour Relations (Consolidation) Act 1992,
    F13. (e)...............................
    (f) M2 the Employment Rights Act 1996 F14[F15...
    [(fg)F16...............................]
    [F17. (g)this Act,]
    (ga) the National Minimum Wage Act 1998,
    (gb) the Employment Relations Act 1999,]
    [F18. (gc)the Equality Act 2006,]
    [F19. (gd)the Pensions Act 2008,]
    [F20. (ge)the Equality Act 2010,]
    [F21. (h)the Working Time Regulations 1998, F22...
    (i) the Transnational Information and Consultation of Employees Regulations 1999]F23[F24...
    (j) the Part-time Workers (Prevention of Less Favourable Treatment) Regulations 2000]F25[F26...
    (k) the Fixed-term Employees (Prevention of Less Favourable Treatment) Regulations 2002]F27[F28...
    (l) F29...............................]
    [F30. (m)F31...............................]

39

[F32. (n)the Merchant Shipping (Working Time: Inland Waterways) Regulations 2003]F33[F34...
(o) the European Public Limited-Liability Company Regulations 2004]
[F35[F36. (p)]the Fishing Vessels (Working Time: Sea-fishermen) Regulations 2004]F37[F38...
(q) the Information and Consultation of Employees Regulations 2004][F39, F40...
(r) the Schedule to the Occupational and Personal Pension Schemes (Consultation by Employers and Miscellaneous Amendment) Regulations 2006]F41[F42...
(s) F43...............................]
[F44. (t)the European Cooperative Society (Involvement of Employees) Regulations 2006 F45[F46...
(u) the Companies (Cross-Border Mergers) Regulations 2007.][F47, F48...
(v) the Cross-border Railway Services (Working Time) Regulations 2008][F49, F50...
(w) the European Public Limited-Liability Company (Employee Involvement) (Great Britain) Regulations 2009. (S.I. 2009/2401).][F51, F52...
(x) the Employment Relations Act 1999 (Blacklists) Regulations 2010.][F53, F54...
(y) the Agency Workers Regulations 2010.] [F55, or]
[F56. (z)the Merchant Shipping (Hours of Work) Regulations 2002.]
(2) No appeal shall lie except to the Appeal Tribunal from any decision of an [F11employment tribunal] under or by virtue of the Acts listed [F57or the Regulations referred to] in subsection (1).
(3) Subsection (1) does not affect any provision contained in, or made under, any Act which provides for an appeal to lie to the Appeal Tribunal (whether from an [F11employment tribunal], the Certification Officer or any other person or body) otherwise than on a question to which that subsection applies.
[F58. (4)The Appeal Tribunal also has any jurisdiction in respect of matters other than appeals which is conferred on it by or under—
(a) the Trade Union and Labour Relations (Consolidation) Act 1992,
(b) this Act, or
(c) any other Act.]]

Amendments (Textual)
F11. Words in s. 21 substituted (1.8.1998) by 1998 c. 8, s. 1. (2)(a) (with s. 16. (2)); S.I. 1998/1658, art. 2. (1), Sch. 1
F12. S. 21. (1)(a)(b)(c) repealed by Equality Act 2010 (c. 15), Sch. 26 Pt. 1 para. 32. (a), Sch. 27 Pt 1 (as amended) (1.10.2010) by S.I. 2010/2279, art. 1. (2), Sch. 1 para. 5, Sch. 2 (see S.I. 2010/2317, art. 2)
F13. S. 21. (1)(e) repealed by Equality Act 2010 (c. 15), Sch. 26 Pt. 1 para. 32. (a), Sch. 27 Pt 1 (as amended) (1.10.2010) by S.I. 2010/2279, art. 1. (2), Sch. 1 para. 5, Sch. 2 (see S.I. 2010/2317, art. 2)
F14. Word at the end of s. 21. (1)(f) repealed (1.11.1998) by 1998 c. 39, s. 53, Sch. 3 (with s. 36); S.I. 1998/2574, art. 2. (1), Sch. 1
F15. S. 21. (1)(g) and word "or" immediately preceding inserted (retrospectively) by 1998 c. 8, ss. 15, 17. (3), Sch. 1 para. 17. (1)(2)
F16. S. 21. (1)(fg) inserted (5.10.1999) by 1999 c. 10, ss. 7, 19. (4), 20. (2), Sch. 3 para. 5, Sch. 6 and repealed (6.4.2003) by 2002 c. 21, ss. 60, 61, Sch. 6; S.I. 2003/962, art. 2. (3)(e), Sch. 1 (subject to arts. 3, 4)
F17. S. 21. (1)(g)(ga)(gb) substituted (1.10.2004) for s. 21. (1)(ff)(g) by Employment Relations Act 2004 (c. 24), ss. 38, 59; S.I. 2004/2566, art. 3. (a)
F18. S. 21. (1)(gc) inserted (30.4.2007) by Equality Act 2006 (c. 3), ss. 40, 93, Sch. 3 para. 57; S.I. 2007/1092, art. 2. (e)
F19. S. 21. (1)(gd) inserted (30.6.2012) by Pensions Act 2008 (c. 30), ss. 59, 149. (1); S.I. 2012/1682, art. 2, Sch. 2
F20. S. 21. (1)(ge) inserted by Equality Act 2010 (c. 15), Sch. 26 Pt. 1 para. 32. (b) (as amended) (1.10.2010) by S.I. 2010/2279, art. 1. (2), Sch. 1 para. 5 (see S.I. 2010/2317, art. 2)

F21. S. 21. (1)(h)(i) substituted (15.1.2000) for words at the end of subsection (1) by S.I. 1999/3323, reg. 35. (3)

F22. Word at the end of s. 21. (1)(h) omitted (1.7.2000) by virtue of S.I. 2000/1551, reg. 10, Sch. para. 1. (b)(i)

F23. Word at the end of s. 21. (1)(i) omitted (1.10.2002) by virtue of S.I. 2002/2034, reg. 11 Sch. 2 para. 2. (b)(i)

F24. S. 21. (1)(j) and word "or" immediately preceding it inserted (1.7.2000) by S.I. 2000/1551, reg. 10, Sch. para. 1. (b)(ii)

F25. Word at the end of s. 21. (1)(j) omitted (1.12.2003) by virtue of The Employment Equality (Sexual Orientation) Regulations 2003 (S.I. 2003/1661), reg. 39, Sch. 5 para. 1. (b)(i)

F26. S. 21. (1)(k) inserted (1.10.2002) by S.I. 2002/2034, reg. 11 Sch. 2 para. 2. (b)(ii)

F27. Word at the end of s. 21. (1)(k) omitted (2.12.2003) by virtue of The Employment Equality (Religion or Belief) Regulations 2003 (S.I. 2003/1660), reg. 39. (2), Sch. 5 para. 1. (b)(i)

F28. S. 21. (1)(l) and preceding word inserted (1.12.2003) by The Employment Equality (Sexual Orientation) Regulations 2003 (S.I. 2003/1661), reg. 39, Sch. 5 para. 1. (b)(ii)

F29. S. 21. (1)(l) repealed by Equality Act 2010 (c. 15), Sch. 26 Pt. 1 para. 32. (a), Sch. 27 Pt 1 (as amended) (1.10.2010) by S.I. 2010/2279, art. 1. (2), Sch. 1 para. 5, Sch. 2 (see S.I. 2010/2317, art. 2)

F30. S. 21. (1)(m) and preceding word inserted (2.12.2003) by The Employment Equality (Religion or Belief) Regulations 2003 (S.I. 2003/1660), reg. 39. (2), Sch. 5 para. 1. (b)(ii)

F31. S. 21. (1)(m) repealed by Equality Act 2010 (c. 15), Sch. 26 Pt. 1 para. 32. (a), Sch. 27 Pt 1 (as amended) (1.10.2010) by S.I. 2010/2279, art. 1. (2), Sch. 1 para. 5, Sch. 2 (see S.I. 2010/2317, art. 2)

F32. S. 21. (1)(n) inserted (24.12.2003) by The Merchant Shipping (Working Time: Inland Waterways) Regulations 2003 (S.I. 2003/3049), reg. 20, Sch. 2 para. 2. (3)

F33. Word at the end of s. 21. (1)(n) repealed (6.4.2005) by The Information and Consultation of Employees Regulations 2004 (S.I. 2004/3426), reg. 37. (a) (with reg. 3)

F34. S. 21. (1)(o) and preceding word inserted (8.10.2004) by The European Public Limited-Liability Company Regulations 2004 (S.I. 2004/2326), reg. 49

F35. S. 21. (1)(o) inserted (16.8.2004) by The Fishing Vessels (Working Time: Sea-fishermen) Regulations 2004 (S.I. 2004/1713), reg. 22, Sch. 2 para.1. (3)

F36. S. 21. (1)(o) renumbered (6.4.2005) as s. 21. (1)(p) by virtue of The Information and Consultation of Employees Regulations 2004 (S.I. 2004/3426), reg. 37. (b) (with reg. 3)

F37. Word at the end of s. 21. (1)(p) omitted (6.4.2006) by virtue of The Occupational and Personal Pension Schemes (Consultation by Employers and Miscellaneous Amendment) Regulations 2006 (S.I. 2006/349), reg. 17, Sch. para. 10. (a) (with reg. 3)

F38. S. 21. (1)(q) and preceding word inserted (6.4.2004) by The Information and Consultation of Employees Regulations 2004 (S.I. 2004/3426), reg. 37. (c) (with reg. 3)

F39. S. 21. (1)(r) and preceding word inserted (6.4.2006) by The Occupational and Personal Pension Schemes (Consultation by Employers and Miscellaneous Amendment) Regulations 2006 (S.I. 2006/349), reg. 17, Sch. para. 10. (b) (with reg. 3)

F40. Word at the end of s. 21. (1)(q) omitted (1.10.2006) by virtue of The Employment Equality (Age) Regulations 2006 (S.I. 2006/1031), reg. 49. (1), Sch. 8 para. 20. (2) (with reg. 44)

F41. Word at the end of s. 21. (1)(r) omitted (18.8.2006) by virtue of The European Cooperative Society (Involvement of Employees) Regulations 2006 (S.I. 2006/2059), reg. 38. (a)

F42. S. 21. (1)(s) and preceding word inserted (1.10.2006) by The Employment Equality (Age) Regulations 2006 (S.I. 2006/1031), reg. 49. (1), Sch. 8 para. 20. (3) (with reg. 44)

F43. S. 21. (1)(s) repealed by Equality Act 2010 (c. 15), Sch. 26 Pt. 1 para. 32. (a), Sch. 27 Pt 1 (as amended) (1.10.2010) by S.I. 2010/2279, art. 1. (2), Sch. 1 para. 5, Sch. 2 (see S.I. 2010/2317, art. 2)

F44. S. 21. (1)(t) and preceding word inserted (18.8.2006) by The European Cooperative Society (Involvement of Employees) Regulations 2006 (S.I. 2006/2059), reg. 38. (b)

F45. Word in s. 21. (1)(t) omitted (27.7.2008) by virtue of The Cross-border Railway Services

(Working Time) Regulations 2008 (S.I. 2008/1660), reg. 1. (1), Sch. 3 para. 1. (b)(i)
F46. S. 21. (1)(u) and preceding word inserted (15.12.2007) by The Companies (Cross-Border Mergers) Regulations 2007 (S.I. 2007/2974), reg. 59. (b)
F47. S. 21. (1)(v) and word inserted (27.7.2008) by The Cross-border Railway Services (Working Time) Regulations 2008 (S.I. 2008/1660), reg. 1. (1), Sch. 3 para. 1. (b)(ii)
F48. Word in s. 21. (1) omitted (1.10.2009) by virtue of The European Public Limited-Liability Company (Employee Involvement) (Great Britain) Regulations 2009 (S.I. 2009/2401), regs. 1. (2), 36 (with regs. 4, 41)
F49. S. 21. (1)(w) and word inserted (1.10.2009) by The European Public Limited-Liability Company (Employee Involvement) (Great Britain) Regulations 2009 (S.I. 2009/2401), regs. 1. (2), 36 (with regs. 4, 41)
F50. Word in s. 21. (1)(v) omitted (2.3.2010) by virtue of The Employment Relations Act 1999 (Blacklists) Regulations 2010 (S.I. 2010/493), regs. 1. (b), 17. (5)(a)
F51. S. 21. (1)(x) and word inserted (2.3.2010) by The Employment Relations Act 1999 (Blacklists) Regulations 2010 (S.I. 2010/493), regs. 1. (b), 17. (5)(b)
F52. Word in s. 21. (1)(w) omitted (1.10.2011) by virtue of The Agency Workers Regulations 2010 (S.I. 2010/93), reg. 1. (1), Sch. 2 para. 8. (b)(i)
F53. S. 21. (1)(y) and word inserted (1.10.2011) by The Agency Workers Regulations 2010 (S.I. 2010/93), reg. 1. (1), Sch. 2 para. 8. (b)(ii)
F54. Word in s. 21. (1)(x) omitted (17.3.2014) by virtue of The Merchant Shipping (Maritime Labour Convention) (Hours of Work) (Amendment) Regulations 2014 (S.I. 2014/308), reg. 1. (2), Sch. para. 1. (3)(a)
F55. Word in s. 21. (1)(y) inserted (17.3.2014) by The Merchant Shipping (Maritime Labour Convention) (Hours of Work) (Amendment) Regulations 2014 (S.I. 2014/308), reg. 1. (2), Sch. para. 1. (3)(b)
F56. S. 21. (1)(z) inserted (17.3.2014) by The Merchant Shipping (Maritime Labour Convention) (Hours of Work) (Amendment) Regulations 2014 (S.I. 2014/308), reg. 1. (2), Sch. para. 1. (3)(c)
F57. Words in s. 21. (2) inserted (1.10.1998) by S.I. 1998/1833, reg. 34. (b)
F58. S. 21. (4) inserted (1.8.1998) by 1998 c. 8, s. 15, Sch. 1 para. 17. (3); S.I. 1998/1658, art. 2. (1), Sch. 1
Marginal Citations
M1 1992 c.52
M2 1996 c.18

Membership etc.

22 Membership of Appeal Tribunal.

(1) The Appeal Tribunal shall consist of—
　(a) such number of judges as may be nominated from time to time [F59 by the Lord Chief Justice, after consulting the Lord Chancellor,] from the judges F60. . . of the High Court and the Court of Appeal [F61 and the judges within subsection (2. A)] ,
　(b) at least one judge of the Court of Session nominated from time to time by the Lord President of the Court of Session, and
　(c) such number of other members as may be appointed from time to time by Her Majesty on the joint recommendation of the Lord Chancellor and the Secretary of State ("appointed members").
(2) The appointed members shall be persons who appear to the Lord Chancellor and the Secretary of State to have special knowledge or experience of industrial relations either—
　(a) as representatives of employers, or
　(b) as representatives of workers (within the meaning of the M3. Trade Union and Labour

Relations (Consolidation) Act 1992).
[F62. (2. A)A person is a judge within this subsection if the person—
  (a) is the Senior President of Tribunals,
  (b) is a deputy judge of the High Court,
  (c) is the Judge Advocate General,
  (d) is a Circuit judge,
  (e) is a Chamber President, or a Deputy Chamber President, of a chamber of the Upper Tribunal or of a chamber of the First-tier Tribunal,
  (f) is a judge of the Upper Tribunal by virtue of appointment under paragraph 1. (1) of Schedule 3 to the Tribunals, Courts and Enforcement Act 2007,
  (g) is a transferred-in judge of the Upper Tribunal (see section 31. (2) of that Act),
  (h) is a deputy judge of the Upper Tribunal (whether under paragraph 7 of Schedule 3 to, or section 31. (2) of, that Act),
  (i) is a district judge, which here does not include a deputy district judge, or
  (j) is a District Judge (Magistrates' Courts), which here does not include a Deputy District Judge (Magistrates' Courts).]
(3) The [F63. Lord Chief Justice shall] appoint one of the judges nominated under subsection (1) to be the President of the Appeal Tribunal.
[F64. (3. A)The Lord Chief Justice must not make an appointment under subsection (3) unless—
  (a) he has consulted the Lord Chancellor, and
  (b) the Lord President of the Court of Session agrees.]
(4) No judge shall be nominated a member of the Appeal Tribunal [F65 under subsection (1)(b)] except with his consent.
[F66. (5)The Lord Chief Justice may nominate a judicial office holder (as defined in section 109. (4) of the Constitutional Reform Act 2005) to exercise his functions under this section.
(6) The Lord President of the Court of Session may nominate a judge of the Court of Session who is a member of the First or Second Division of the Inner House of that Court to exercise his functions under subsection (3. A)(b).]

Amendments (Textual)
F59. Words in s. 22. (1)(a) substituted (3.4.2006) by Constitutional Reform Act 2005 (c. 4), ss. 15, 148, Sch. 4 para. 246. (2)(a); S.I. 2006/1014, art. 2. (a), Sch. 1
F60. Words in s. 22. (1)(a) repealed (3.4.2006) by Constitutional Reform Act 2005 (c. 4), ss. 15, 146, 148, Sch. 4 para. 246. (2)(b), Sch. 18 Pt. 2; S.I. 2006/1014, art. 2. (a), Sch. 1
F61. Words in s. 22. (1)(a) inserted (1.10.2013) by Crime and Courts Act 2013 (c. 22), s. 61. (3), Sch. 14 para. 11. (2); S.I. 2013/2200, art. 3. (g)
F62. S. 22. (2. A) inserted (1.10.2013) by Crime and Courts Act 2013 (c. 22), s. 61. (3), Sch. 14 para. 11. (3); S.I. 2013/2200, art. 3. (g)
F63. Words in s. 22. (3) substituted (3.4.2006) by Constitutional Reform Act 2005 (c. 4), ss. 15, 148, Sch. 4 para. 246. (3); S.I. 2006/1014, art. 2. (a), Sch. 1
F64. S. 22. (3. A) inserted (3.4.2006) by Constitutional Reform Act 2005 (c. 4), ss. 15, 148, Sch. 4 para. 246. (4); S.I. 2006/1014, art. 2. (a), Sch. 1
F65. Words in s. 22. (4) inserted (1.10.2013) by Crime and Courts Act 2013 (c. 22), s. 61. (3), Sch. 14 para. 11. (4); S.I. 2013/2200, art. 3. (g)
F66. S. 22. (5)(6) inserted (3.4.2006) by Constitutional Reform Act 2005 (c. 4), ss. 15, 148, Sch. 4 para. 246. (5); S.I. 2006/1014, art. 2. (a), Sch. 1

Marginal Citations
M31992 c. 52.

23 Temporary membership.

(1) At any time when—
  (a) the office of President of the Appeal Tribunal is vacant, or

(b) the person holding that office is temporarily absent or otherwise unable to act as the President of the Appeal Tribunal,

the [F67. Lord Chief Justice] may nominate another judge nominated under section 22. (1)(a) to act temporarily in his place.

(2) At any time when a judge of the Appeal Tribunal nominated under paragraph (a) or (b) of subsection (1) of section 22 is temporarily absent or otherwise unable to act as a member of the Appeal Tribunal—

(a) in the case of a judge nominated under paragraph (a) of that subsection, the [F68. Lord Chief Justice] may nominate another judge who is qualified to be nominated under that paragraph to act temporarily in his place, and

(b) in the case of a judge nominated under paragraph (b) of that subsection, the Lord President of the Court of Session may nominate another judge who is qualified to be nominated under that paragraph to act temporarily in his place.

(3) At any time when an appointed member of the Appeal Tribunal is temporarily absent or otherwise unable to act as a member of the Appeal Tribunal, the Lord Chancellor and the Secretary of State may jointly appoint a person appearing to them to have the qualifications for appointment as an appointed member to act temporarily in his place.

(4) A person nominated or appointed to act temporarily in place of the President or any other member of the Appeal Tribunal, when so acting, has all the functions of the person in whose place he acts.

(5) No judge shall be nominated to act temporarily as a member of the Appeal Tribunal except with his consent.

[F69. (6)The functions conferred on the Lord Chief Justice by the preceding provisions of this section may be exercised only after consulting the Lord Chancellor.

(7) The functions conferred on the Lord Chancellor by subsection (3) may be exercised only after consultation with the Lord Chief Justice.

(8) The Lord Chief Justice may nominate a judicial office holder (as defined in section 109. (4) of the Constitutional Reform Act 2005) to exercise his functions under this section.]

Amendments (Textual)

F67. Words in s. 23. (1) substituted (3.4.2006) by Constitutional Reform Act 2005 (c. 4), ss. 15, 148, Sch. 4 para. 247. (2); S.I. 2006/1014, art. 2. (a), Sch. 1

F68. Words in s. 23. (2)(a) substituted (3.4.2006) by Constitutional Reform Act 2005 (c. 4), ss. 15, 148, Sch. 4 para. 247. (3); S.I. 2006/1014, art. 2. (a), Sch. 1

F69. S. 23. (6)-(8) inserted (3.4.2006) by Constitutional Reform Act 2005 (c. 4), ss. 15, 148, Sch. 4 para. 247. (4); S.I. 2006/1014, art. 2. (a), Sch. 1

24 Temporary additional judicial membership.

[F70. (1)This section applies if both of the following conditions are met—

(a) the Lord Chancellor thinks that it is expedient, after consulting the Lord Chief Justice, for a qualified person to be appointed to be a temporary additional judge of the Appeal Tribunal in order to facilitate in England and Wales the disposal of business in the Appeal Tribunal;

(b) the Lord Chancellor requests the Lord Chief Justice to make such an appointment.

(1. A)The Lord Chief Justice may, after consulting the Lord Chancellor, appoint a qualified person as mentioned in subsection (1)(a).

(1. B)An appointment under this section is—

(a) for such period, or

(b) on such occasions,

as the Lord Chief Justice determines, after consulting the Lord Chancellor.]

(2) In [F71this section]"qualified person" means a person who—

(a) is qualified for appointment as a judge of the High Court under section 10 of the M4. Supreme Court Act 1981, or

(b) has held office as a judge of the High Court or the Court of Appeal.
(3) A person appointed to be a temporary additional judge of the Appeal Tribunal has all the functions of a judge nominated under section 22. (1)(a).
[F72. (4)The Lord Chief Justice may nominate a judicial office holder (as defined in section 109. (4) of the Constitutional Reform Act 2005) to exercise his functions under this section.]
Amendments (Textual)
F70. S. 24. (1)-(1. B) substituted (3.4.2006) for s. 24. (1) by Constitutional Reform Act 2005 (c. 4), ss. 15, 148, Sch. 4 para. 248. (2); S.I. 2006/1014, art. 2. (a), Sch. 1
F71. Words in s. 24. (2) substituted (3.4.2006) by Constitutional Reform Act 2005 (c. 4), ss. 15, 148, Sch. 4 para. 248. (3); S.I. 2006/1014, art. 2. (a), Sch. 1
F72. S. 24. (4) inserted (3.4.2006) by Constitutional Reform Act 2005 (c. 4), ss. 15, 148, Sch. 4 para. 248. (4); S.I. 2006/1014, art. 2. (a), Sch. 1
Marginal Citations
M41981 c. 54.

[F7324. ATraining etc. of members of Appeal Tribunal

The Senior President of Tribunals is responsible, within the resources made available by the Lord Chancellor, for the maintenance of appropriate arrangements for the training, guidance and welfare of judges, and other members, of the Appeal Tribunal (in their capacities as members of the Appeal Tribunal).
Amendments (Textual)
F73. Ss. 24. A, 24. B inserted (3.11.2008) by Tribunals, Courts and Enforcement Act 2007 (c. 15), s. 148, Sch. 8 para. 44; S.I. 2008/2696, art. 5. (c)(i) (with art. 3)

24. BOaths

(1) Subsection (2) applies to a person ("the appointee")—
    (a) who is appointed under section 22. (1)(c) or 23. (3), or
    (b) who is appointed under section 24. (1. A) and—
(i) falls when appointed within paragraph (a), but not paragraph (b), of section 24. (2), and
(ii) has not previously taken the required oaths after accepting another office.
(2) The appointee must take the required oaths before—
    (a) the Senior President of Tribunals, or
    (b) an eligible person who is nominated by the Senior President of Tribunals for the purpose of taking the oaths from the appointee.
(3) If the appointee is a member of the Appeal Tribunal appointed before the coming into force of this section, the requirement in subsection (2) applies in relation to the appointee from the coming into force of this section.
(4) A person is eligible for the purposes of subsection (2)(b) if one or more of the following paragraphs applies to him—
    (a) he holds high judicial office (as defined in section 60. (2) of the Constitutional Reform Act 2005);
    (b) he holds judicial office (as defined in section 109. (4) of that Act);
    (c) he holds (in Scotland) the office of sheriff.
(5) In this section "the required oaths" means—
    (a) the oath of allegiance, and
    (b) the judicial oath,
as set out in the Promissory Oaths Act 1868.]
Amendments (Textual)
F73. Ss. 24. A, 24. B inserted (3.11.2008) by Tribunals, Courts and Enforcement Act 2007 (c. 15), s. 148, Sch. 8 para. 44; S.I. 2008/2696, art. 5. (c)(i) (with art. 3)

25 Tenure of appointed members.

(1) Subject to subsections (2) to (4), an appointed member shall hold and vacate office in accordance with the terms of his appointment.
(2) An appointed member—
   (a) may at any time resign his membership by notice in writing addressed to the Lord Chancellor and the Secretary of State, and
   (b) shall vacate his office on the day on which he attains the age of seventy.
(3) Subsection (2)(b) is subject to section 26. (4) to (6) of the M5. Judicial Pensions and Retirement Act 1993 (Lord Chancellor's power to authorise continuance of office up to the age of seventy-five).
(4) If the Lord Chancellor, after consultation with the Secretary of State, is satisfied that an appointed member—
   (a) has been absent from sittings of the Appeal Tribunal for a period longer than six consecutive months without the permission of the President of the Appeal Tribunal,
   (b) has become bankrupt or [F74had a debt relief order (under Part 7. A of the Insolvency Act 1986) made in respect of him or has] made an arrangement with his creditors, or has had his estate sequestrated or made a trust deed for behoof of his creditors or a composition contract,
   (c) is incapacitated by physical or mental illness, or
   (d) is otherwise unable or unfit to discharge the functions of a member,
the Lord Chancellor may declare his office as a member to be vacant and shall notify the declaration in such manner as the Lord Chancellor thinks fit; and when the Lord Chancellor does so, the office becomes vacant.
[F75. (5)The Lord Chancellor may declare an appointed member's office vacant under subsection (4) only with the concurrence of the appropriate senior judge.
(6) The appropriate senior judge is the Lord Chief Justice of England and Wales, unless the member whose office is to be declared vacant exercises functions wholly or mainly in Scotland, in which case it is the Lord President of the Court of Session.]
Amendments (Textual)
F74. Words in s. 25. (4)(b) inserted (1.10.2012) by The Tribunals, Courts and Enforcement Act 2007 (Consequential Amendments) Order 2012 (S.I. 2012/2404), art. 1, Sch. 2 para. 35 (with art. 5)
F75. S. 25. (5)(6) inserted (3.4.2006) by Constitutional Reform Act 2005 (c. 4), ss. 15, 148, Sch. 4 para. 249; S.I. 2006/1014, art. 2. (a), Sch. 1
Marginal Citations
M51993 c. 8.

F7626 Staff.

. . . .
Amendments (Textual)
F76. S. 26 repealed (3.11.2008) by Tribunals, Courts and Enforcement Act 2007 (c. 15), s. 148, Sch. 23 Pt. 1; S.I. 2008/2696, art. 5. (i) (with art. 3)

27 Remuneration, pensions and allowances.

(1) The Secretary of State shall pay—
   (a) the appointed members, [F77 and]
   (b) any person appointed to act temporarily in the place of an appointed member, F78...
   F79. (c). . . . .

such remuneration and such travelling and other allowances as he may, with the relevant approval, determine; and for this purpose the relevant approval is that of the Treasury in the case of persons within paragraph (a) or (b)F80....

(2) A person appointed to be a temporary additional judge of the Appeal Tribunal shall be paid such remuneration and allowances as the Lord Chancellor may, with the approval of the Treasury, determine.

(3) If the Secretary of State determines, with the approval of the Treasury, that this subsection applies in the case of an appointed member, the Secretary of State shall—

(a) pay such pension, allowance or gratuity to or in respect of that person on his retirement or death, or

(b) make to the member such payments towards the provision of a pension, allowance or gratuity for his retirement or death,

as the Secretary of State may, with the approval of the Treasury, determine.

(4) Where—

(a) a person ceases to be an appointed member otherwise than on his retirement or death, and

(b) it appears to the Secretary of State that there are special circumstances which make it right for him to receive compensation,

the Secretary of State may make to him a payment of such amount as the Secretary of State may, with the approval of the Treasury, determine.

Amendments (Textual)

F77. Word in s. 27. (1)(a) inserted (3.11.2008) by Tribunals, Courts and Enforcement Act 2007 (c. 15), s. 148, Sch. 8 para. 45; S.I. 2008/2696, art. 5. (c)(i) (with art. 3)

F78. Word in s. 27. (1)(b) repealed (3.11.2008) by Tribunals, Courts and Enforcement Act 2007 (c. 15), s. 148, Sch. 23 Pt. 1; S.I. 2008/2696, art. 5. (i) (with art. 3)

F79. S. 27. (1)(c) repealed (3.11.2008) by Tribunals, Courts and Enforcement Act 2007 (c. 15), s. 148, Sch. 23 Pt. 1; S.I. 2008/2696, art. 5. (i) (with art. 3)

F80. Words in s. 27. (1) repealed (3.11.2008) by Tribunals, Courts and Enforcement Act 2007 (c. 15), s. 148, Sch. 23 Pt. 1; S.I. 2008/2696, art. 5. (i) (with art. 3)

28 Composition of Appeal Tribunal.

(1) The Appeal Tribunal may sit, in accordance with directions given by the President of the Appeal Tribunal, either as a single tribunal or in two or more divisions concurrently.

(2) Subject to subsections (3) to (5), proceedings before the Appeal Tribunal shall be heard by a judge and either two or four appointed members, so that in either case there is an equal number—

(a) of persons whose knowledge or experience of industrial relations is as representatives of employers, and

(b) of persons whose knowledge or experience of industrial relations is as representatives of workers.

(3) With the consent of the parties, proceedings before the Appeal Tribunal may be heard by a judge and one appointed member or by a judge and three appointed members.

(4) Proceedings on an appeal on a [F81chairman-alone question] shall be heard by a judge alone unless a judge directs that the proceedings shall be heard in accordance with subsections (2) and (3).

[F82. (4. A)In subsection (4) "chairman-alone question" means—

(a) a question arising from any decision of an employment tribunal that is a decision of—

(i) the person mentioned in section 4. (1)(a) acting alone, or

(ii) any Employment Judge acting alone, or

(b) a question arising in any proceedings before an employment tribunal that are proceedings before—

(i) the person mentioned in section 4. (1)(a) alone, or

(ii) any Employment Judge alone.]

F83. (5). . . . .

Amendments (Textual)

F81. Words in s. 28. (4) substituted (3.11.2008) by Tribunals, Courts and Enforcement Act 2007 (c. 15), s. 148, Sch. 8 para. 46. (2); S.I. 2008/2696, art. 5. (c)(i) (with art. 3)

F82. S. 28. (4. A) inserted (3.11.2008) by Tribunals, Courts and Enforcement Act 2007 (c. 15), s. 148, Sch. 8 para. 46. (3); S.I. 2008/2696, art. 5. (c)(i) (with art. 3)

F83. S. 28. (5) repealed (16.7.2001) by 1999 c. 26, ss. 41, 44, Sch. 8 para. 4, Sch. 9. (12); S.I. 2001/1187, art. 3. (b), Sch. (as amended by S.I. 2001/1461, art. 2. (2))

Procedure

29 Conduct of hearings.

(1) A person may appear before the Appeal Tribunal in person or be represented by—
  (a) counsel or a solicitor,
  (b) a representative of a trade union or an employers' association, or
  (c) any other person whom he desires to represent him.
(2) The Appeal Tribunal has in relation to—
  (a) the attendance and examination of witnesses,
  (b) the production and inspection of documents, and
  (c) all other matters incidental to its jurisdiction,
the same powers, rights, privileges and authority (in England and Wales) as the High Court and (in Scotland) as the Court of Session.

[F8429. APractice directions

(1) Directions about the procedure of the Appeal Tribunal may be given—
  (a) by the Senior President of Tribunals, or
  (b) by the President of the Appeal Tribunal.
(2) A power under subsection (1) includes—
  (a) power to vary or revoke directions given in exercise of the power, and
  (b) power to make different provision for different purposes.
(3) Directions under subsection (1)(a) may not be given without the approval of the Lord Chancellor.
(4) Directions under subsection (1)(b) may not be given without the approval of—
  (a) the Senior President of Tribunals, and
  (b) the Lord Chancellor.
(5) Subsection (1) does not prejudice any power apart from that subsection to give directions about the procedure of the Appeal Tribunal.
(6) Directions may not be given in exercise of any such power as is mentioned in subsection (5) without the approval of—
  (a) the Senior President of Tribunals, and
  (b) the Lord Chancellor.
(7) Subsections (3), (4)(b) and (6)(b) do not apply to directions to the extent that they consist of guidance about any of the following—
  (a) the application or interpretation of the law;
  (b) the making of decisions by members of the Appeal Tribunal.
(8) Subsections (3), (4)(b) and (6)(b) do not apply to directions to the extent that they consist of criteria for determining which members of the Appeal Tribunal may be chosen to decide particular categories of matter; but the directions may, to that extent, be given only after consulting the Lord

Chancellor.
(9) Subsections (4) and (6) do not apply to directions given in a particular case for the purposes of that case only.
(10) Subsection (6) does not apply to directions under section 28. (1).]
Amendments (Textual)
F84. S. 29. A inserted (3.11.2008) by Tribunals, Courts and Enforcement Act 2007 (c. 15), s. 148, Sch. 8 para. 47; S.I. 2008/2696, art. 5. (c)(i) (with art. 3)

30 Appeal Tribunal procedure rules.

(1) The Lord Chancellor, after consultation with the Lord President of the Court of Session, shall make rules ("Appeal Tribunal procedure rules") with respect to proceedings before the Appeal Tribunal.
(2) Appeal Tribunal procedure rules may, in particular, include provision—
    (a) with respect to the manner in which, and the time within which, an appeal may be brought,
    (b) with respect to the manner in which [F85or complaint] to the Appeal Tribunal may be made,
    (c) for requiring persons to attend to give evidence and produce documents and for authorising the administration of oaths to witnesses,
    (d) for requiring or enabling the Appeal Tribunal to sit in private in circumstances in which an [F86employment tribunal] is required or empowered to sit in private by virtue of [F87section 10. A] of this Act,
    (e) F88. . . . .
    (f) for interlocutory matters arising on any appeal or application to the Appeal Tribunal to be dealt with [F89 by an officer of the Appeal Tribunal] .
[F90. (2. A)Appeal Tribunal procedure rules may make provision of a kind which may be made by employment tribunal procedure regulations under section 10. (2), (5), (6) or (7).
(2. B)For the purposes of subsection (2. A)—
    (a) the reference in section 10. (2) to section 4 shall be treated as a reference to section 28, and
    (b) the reference in section 10. (4) to the President or a Regional [F91 Employment Judge] shall be treated as a reference to a judge of the Appeal Tribunal.
(2. C)Section 10. B shall have effect in relation to a direction to or determination of the Appeal Tribunal as it has effect in relation to a direction to or determination of an employment tribunal.]
(3) Subject to Appeal Tribunal procedure rules [F92 and directions under section 28. (1) or 29. A(1)] , the Appeal Tribunal has power to regulate its own procedure.
Amendments (Textual)
F85. Words in s. 30. (2)(b) substituted (15.1.2000) by S.I. 1999/3323, reg. 35. (4)
F86. Words in s. 30 (2)(d) substituted (1.8.1998) by 1998 c. 8, s. 1. (2)(a) (with s. 16. (2)); S.I. 1998/1658, art. 2. (1), Sch. 1
F87. Words in s. 30. (2)(d) substituted (16.7.2001) by 1999 c. 26, ss. 41, 45. (1), Sch. 8 para. 5; S.I. 2001/1187, art. 3. (b), Sch. (as amended by S.I. 2001/1461, art. 2. (2))
F88. S. 30. (2)(e) omitted (31.12.2004) by virtue of Employment Relations Act 2004 (c. 24), ss. 57, 59. (2)-(4), Sch. 1 para. 26; and the said s. 30. (2)(e) repealed (6.4.2005) by {Sch. 2} of the said Employment Relations Act 2004 (c. 24); S.I. 2004/3342, art. 4. (b) (with arts. 5-12); S.I. 2005/872, art. 4, Sch (with arts. 5-21)
F89. Words in s. 30. (2)(f) substituted (25.6.2013) by Enterprise and Regulatory Reform Act 2013 (c. 24), ss. 12. (3), 103. (2) (with s. 24. (2))
F90. S. 30. (2. A)-(2. C) inserted (16.7.2001) by 1999 c. 26, ss. 41, 45. (1), Sch. 8 para. 5; S.I. 2001/1187, art. 3. (b), Sch. (as amended by S.I. 2001/1461, art. 2. (2))
F91. Words in s. 30. (2. B)(b) substituted (1.10.2013) by Crime and Courts Act 2013 (c. 22), s. 61. (3), Sch. 14 para. 13. (3); S.I. 2013/2200, art. 3. (g)
F92. Words in s. 30. (3) inserted (3.11.2008) by Tribunals, Courts and Enforcement Act 2007 (c. 15), s. 148, Sch. 8 para. 48; S.I. 2008/2696, art. 5. (c)(i) (with art. 3)

31 Restriction of publicity in cases involving sexual misconduct.

(1) Appeal Tribunal procedure rules may, as respects proceedings to which this section applies, include provision—
    (a) for cases involving allegations of the commission of sexual offences, for securing that the registration or other making available of documents or decisions shall be so effected as to prevent the identification of any person affected by or making the allegation, and
    (b) for cases involving allegations of sexual misconduct, enabling the Appeal Tribunal, on the application of any party to the proceedings before it or of its own motion, to make a restricted reporting order having effect (if not revoked earlier) until the promulgation of the decision of the Appeal Tribunal.

(2) This section applies to—
    (a) proceedings on an appeal against a decision of an [F93employment tribunal] to make, or not to make, a restricted reporting order, and
    (b) proceedings on an appeal against any interlocutory decision of an [F93employment tribunal] in proceedings in which the [F93employment tribunal] has made a restricted reporting order which it has not revoked.

(3) If any identifying matter is published or included in a relevant programme in contravention of a restricted reporting order—
    (a) in the case of publication in a newspaper or periodical, any proprietor, any editor and any publisher of the newspaper or periodical,
    (b) in the case of publication in any other form, the person publishing the matter, and
    (c) in the case of matter included in a relevant programme—
(i) any body corporate engaged in providing the service in which the programme is included, and
(ii) any person having functions in relation to the programme corresponding to those of an editor of a newspaper,
shall be guilty of an offence and liable on summary conviction to a fine not exceeding level 5 on the standard scale.

(4) Where a person is charged with an offence under subsection (3) it is a defence to prove that at the time of the alleged offence he was not aware, and neither suspected nor had reason to suspect, that the publication or programme in question was of, or included, the matter in question.

(5) Where an offence under subsection (3) committed by a body corporate is proved to have been committed with the consent or connivance of, or to be attributable to any neglect on the part of—
    (a) a director, manager, secretary or other similar officer of the body corporate, or
    (b) a person purporting to act in any such capacity,
he as well as the body corporate is guilty of the offence and liable to be proceeded against and punished accordingly.

(6) In relation to a body corporate whose affairs are managed by its members "director", in subsection (5), means a member of the body corporate.

(7) "Restricted reporting order" means—
    (a) in subsections (1) and (3), an order—
(i) made in exercise of a power conferred by rules made by virtue of this section, and
(ii) prohibiting the publication in Great Britain of identifying matter in a written publication available to the public or its inclusion in a relevant programme for reception in Great Britain, and
    (b) in subsection (2), an order which is a restricted reporting order for the purposes of section 11.

(8) In this section—
"identifying matter", in relation to a person, means any matter likely to lead members of the public to identify him as a person affected by, or as the person making, the allegation,
"relevant programme" has the same meaning as in the M6. Sexual Offences (Amendment) Act 1992,

"sexual misconduct" means the commission of a sexual offence, sexual harassment or other adverse conduct (of whatever nature) related to sex, and conduct is related to sex whether the relationship with sex lies in the character of the conduct or in its having reference to the sex or sexual orientation of the person at whom the conduct is directed,

"sexual offence" means any offence to which section 4 of the M7. Sexual Offences (Amendment) Act 1976, the Sexual Offences (Amendment) Act 1992 or section 274. (2) of the M8. Criminal Procedure (Scotland) Act 1995 applies (offences under the M9. Sexual Offences Act 1956, Part I of the M10. Criminal Law (Consolidation) (Scotland) Act 1995 and certain other enactments), and "written publication" has the same meaning as in the Sexual Offences (Amendment) Act 1992.

Amendments (Textual)
F93. Words in s. 31. (2) substituted (1.8.1998) by 1998 c. 8, s. 1. (2)(a) (with s. 16. (2)); S.I. 1998/1658, art. 2. (1), Sch. 1

Marginal Citations
M61992 c. 34.
M71976 c. 82.
M81995 c. 46.
M91956 c. 69.
M101995 c. 39.

32 Restriction of publicity in disability cases.

(1) This section applies to proceedings—

(a) on an appeal against a decision of an [F94employment tribunal] to make, or not to make, a restricted reporting order, or

(b) on an appeal against any interlocutory decision of an [F94employment tribunal] in proceedings in which the [F94employment tribunal] has made a restricted reporting order which it has not revoked.

(2) Appeal Tribunal procedure rules may, as respects proceedings to which this section applies, include provision for—

(a) enabling the Appeal Tribunal, on the application of the complainant or of its own motion, to make a restricted reporting order having effect (if not revoked earlier) until the promulgation of the decision of the Appeal Tribunal, and

(b) where a restricted reporting order is made in relation to an appeal which is being dealt with by the Appeal Tribunal together with any other proceedings, enabling the Appeal Tribunal to direct that the order is to apply also in relation to those other proceedings or such part of them as the Appeal Tribunal may direct.

(3) If any identifying matter is published or included in a relevant programme in contravention of a restricted reporting order—

(a) in the case of publication in a newspaper or periodical, any proprietor, any editor and any publisher of the newspaper or periodical,

(b) in the case of publication in any other form, the person publishing the matter, and

(c) in the case of matter included in a relevant programme—

(i) any body corporate engaged in providing the service in which the programme is included, and

(ii) any person having functions in relation to the programme corresponding to those of an editor of a newspaper,

shall be guilty of an offence and liable on summary conviction to a fine not exceeding level 5 on the standard scale.

(4) Where a person is charged with an offence under subsection (3), it is a defence to prove that at the time of the alleged offence he was not aware, and neither suspected nor had reason to suspect, that the publication or programme in question was of, or included, the matter in question.

(5) Where an offence under subsection (3) committed by a body corporate is proved to have been committed with the consent or connivance of, or to be attributable to any neglect on the part of—

(a) a director, manager, secretary or other similar officer of the body corporate, or

(b) a person purporting to act in any such capacity,

he as well as the body corporate is guilty of the offence and liable to be proceeded against and punished accordingly.

(6) In relation to a body corporate whose affairs are managed by its members "director", in subsection (5), means a member of the body corporate.

(7) "Restricted reporting order" means—

(a) in subsection (1), an order which is a restricted reporting order for the purposes of section 12, and

(b) in subsections (2) and (3), an order—

(i) made in exercise of a power conferred by rules made by virtue of this section, and

(ii) prohibiting the publication in Great Britain of identifying matter in a written publication available to the public or its inclusion in a relevant programme for reception in Great Britain.

(8) In this section—

"complainant" means the person who made the complaint to which the proceedings before the Appeal Tribunal relate,

"identifying matter" means any matter likely to lead members of the public to identify the complainant or such other persons (if any) as may be named in the order,

"promulgation" has such meaning as may be prescribed by rules made by virtue of this section,

"relevant programme" means a programme included in a programme service, within the meaning of the M11. Broadcasting Act 1990, and

"written publication" includes a film, a sound track and any other record in permanent form but does not include an indictment or other document prepared for use in particular legal proceedings.

Amendments (Textual)

F94. Words in s. 32. (1) substituted (1.8.1998) by 1998 c. 8, s. 1. (2)(a) (with s. 16. (2)); S.I. 1998/1658, art. 2. (1), Sch. 1

Commencement Information

I1. S. 32 wholly in force at 22.8.1996 with effect as mentioned in Sch. 2 Pt. II para. 7. (7)(8) and S.I. 1996/3150, art. 2

Marginal Citations

M11 1990 c. 42.

33 Restriction of vexatious proceedings.

(1) If, on an application made by the Attorney General or the Lord Advocate under this section, the Appeal Tribunal is satisfied that a person has habitually and persistently and without any reasonable ground—

(a) instituted vexatious proceedings, whether [F95before the Certification Officer,] in an [F96employment tribunal] or before the Appeal Tribunal, and whether against the same person or against different persons, or

(b) made vexatious applications in any proceedings, whether [F97before the Certification Officer,] in an [F96employment tribunal] or before the Appeal Tribunal,

the Appeal Tribunal may, after hearing the person or giving him an opportunity of being heard, make a restriction of proceedings order.

(2) A "restriction of proceedings order" is an order that—

(a) no proceedings shall without the leave of the Appeal Tribunal be instituted [F98before the Certification Officer,] in any [F96employment tribunal] or before the Appeal Tribunal by the person against whom the order is made,

(b) any proceedings instituted by him [F99before the Certification Officer,] in any [F96employment tribunal] or before the Appeal Tribunal before the making of the order shall not be continued by him without the leave of the Appeal Tribunal, and

(c) no application (other than one for leave under this section) is to be made by him in any proceedings [F100before the Certification Officer,] in any [F96employment tribunal] or before the Appeal Tribunal without the leave of the Appeal Tribunal.

(3) A restriction of proceedings order may provide that it is to cease to have effect at the end of a specified period, but otherwise it remains in force indefinitely.

(4) Leave for the institution or continuance of, or for the making of an application in, any proceedings [F101before the Certification Officer,] in an [F96employment tribunal] or before the Appeal Tribunal by a person who is the subject of a restriction of proceedings order shall not be given unless the Appeal Tribunal is satisfied—

(a) that the proceedings or application are not an abuse of the [F102process] , and

(b) that there are reasonable grounds for the proceedings or application.

(5) A copy of a restriction of proceedings order shall be published in the London Gazette and the Edinburgh Gazette.

Amendments (Textual)

F95. Words in s. 33. (1)(a) inserted (6.4.2005) by Employment Relations Act 2004 (c. 24), ss. 49. (2), 59; S. I. 2005/872, art. 4, Sch. (with arts. 5-21)

F96. Words in s. 33. (1)(2)(b)(c)(4) substituted (1.8.1998) by 1998 c. 8, s. 1. (2)(a) (with s. 16. (2)); S.I. 1998/1658, art. 2. (1), Sch. 1

F97. Words in s. 33. (1)(b) inserted (6.4.2005) by Employment Relations Act 2004 (c. 24), ss. 49. (3), 59; S. I. 2005/872, art. 4, Sch. (with arts. 5-21)

F98. Words in s. 33. (2)(a) inserted (6.4.2005) by Employment Relations Act 2004 (c. 24), ss. 49. (4), 59; S. I. 2005/872, art. 4, Sch. (with arts. 5-21)

F99. Words in s. 33. (2)(b) inserted (6.4.2005) by Employment Relations Act 2004 (c. 24), ss. 49. (5), 59; S. I. 2005/872, art. 4, Sch. (with arts. 5-21)

F100. Words in s. 33. (2)(c) inserted (6.4.2005) by Employment Relations Act 2004 (c. 24), ss. 49. (6), 59; S. I. 2005/872, art. 4, Sch. (with arts. 5-21)

F101. Words in s. 33. (4) inserted (6.4.2005) by Employment Relations Act 2004 (c. 24), ss. 49. (7)(a), 59; S. I. 2005/872, art. 4, Sch. (with arts. 5-21)

F102. Words in s. 33. (4) substituted (6.4.2005) by Employment Relations Act 2004 (c. 24), ss. 49. (7)(b), 59; S. I. 2005/872, art. 4, Sch. (with arts. 5-21)

Modifications etc. (not altering text)

C1. S. 33: transfer of functions (6.5.1999) by S.I. 1999/901, arts. 4-8, Sch.

[F10334 Costs and expenses

(1) Appeal Tribunal procedure rules may include provision for the award of costs or expenses.

(2) Rules under subsection (1) may include provision authorising the Appeal Tribunal to have regard to a person's ability to pay when considering the making of an award against him under such rules.

(3) Appeal Tribunal procedure rules may include provision for authorising the Appeal Tribunal—

(a) to disallow all or part of the costs or expenses of a representative of a party to proceedings before it by reason of that representative's conduct of the proceedings;

(b) to order a representative of a party to proceedings before it to meet all or part of the costs or expenses incurred by a party by reason of the representative's conduct of the proceedings.

(4) Appeal Tribunal procedure rules may also include provision for taxing or otherwise settling the costs or expenses referred to in subsection (1) or (3)(b) (and, in particular in England and Wales, for enabling the amount of such costs to be assessed by way of detailed assessment in the High Court).]

Amendments (Textual)

F103. S. 34 substituted (9.7.2004) by 2002 c. 22, ss. 23, 55. (2); S.I. 2004/1717, art. 2. (1)

Decisions and further appeals

35 Powers of Appeal Tribunal.

(1) For the purpose of disposing of an appeal, the Appeal Tribunal may—
   (a) exercise any of the powers of the body or officer from whom the appeal was brought, or
   (b) remit the case to that body or officer.
(2) Any decision or award of the Appeal Tribunal on an appeal has the same effect, and may be enforced in the same manner, as a decision or award of the body or officer from whom the appeal was brought.

36 Enforcement of decisions etc.

(1) F104. . . . .
(2) F104. . . . .
(3) F104. . . . .
(4) No person shall be punished for contempt of the Appeal Tribunal except by, or with the consent of, a judge.
(5) A magistrates' court shall not remit the whole or part of a fine imposed by the Appeal Tribunal unless it has the consent of a judge who is a member of the Appeal Tribunal.
Amendments (Textual)
F104. S. 36. (1)-(3) omitted (31.12.2004) by virtue of Employment Relations Act 2004 (c. 24), ss. 57, 59. (2)-(4), Sch. 1 para. 27; and the said s. 36. (1)-(3) repealed (6.4.2005) by {Sch. 2} of the said Employment Relations Act 2004 (c. 24); S.I. 2004/3342, art. 4. (b) (with arts. 5-12); S.I. 2005/872, art. 4, Sch (with arts. 5-21)

37 Appeals from Appeal Tribunal.

(1) Subject to subsection (3), an appeal on any question of law lies from any decision or order of the Appeal Tribunal to the relevant appeal court with the leave of the Appeal Tribunal or of the relevant appeal court.
(2) In subsection (1) the "relevant appeal court" means—
   (a) in the case of proceedings in England and Wales, the Court of Appeal, and
   (b) in the case of proceedings in Scotland, the Court of Session.
(3) No appeal lies from a decision of the Appeal Tribunal refusing leave for the institution or continuance of, or for the making of an application in, proceedings by a person who is the subject of a restriction of proceedings order made under section 33.
(4) This section is without prejudice to section 13 of the M12. Administration of Justice Act 1960 (appeal in case of contempt of court).
Marginal Citations
M121960 c. 65.

[F10537. ZAAppeals to Supreme Court: grant of certificate by Appeal Tribunal

(1) If the Appeal Tribunal is satisfied that—
   (a) the conditions in subsection (4) or (5) are fulfilled in relation to the Appeal Tribunal's decision or order in any proceedings, and
   (b) as regards that decision or order, a sufficient case for an appeal to the Supreme Court has been made out to justify an application under section 37. ZB,
the Appeal Tribunal may grant a certificate to that effect.
(2) The Appeal Tribunal may grant a certificate under this section only on an application made by

a party to the proceedings.
(3) The Appeal Tribunal may not grant a certificate under this section in the case of proceedings in Scotland.
(4) The conditions in this subsection are that a point of law of general public importance is involved in the decision or order of the Appeal Tribunal and that point of law is—
 (a) a point of law that—
(i) relates wholly or mainly to the construction of an enactment or statutory instrument, and
(ii) has been fully argued in the proceedings and fully considered in the judgment of the Appeal Tribunal in the proceedings, or
 (b) a point of law—
(i) in respect of which the Appeal Tribunal is bound by a decision of the Court of Appeal or the Supreme Court in previous proceedings, and
(ii) that was fully considered in the judgments given by the Court of Appeal or, as the case may be, the Supreme Court in those previous proceedings.
(5) The conditions in this subsection are that a point of law of general public importance is involved in the decision or order of the Appeal Tribunal and that—
 (a) the proceedings entail a decision relating to a matter of national importance or consideration of such a matter,
 (b) the result of the proceedings is so significant (whether considered on its own or together with other proceedings or likely proceedings) that, in the opinion of the Appeal Tribunal, a hearing by the Supreme Court is justified, or
 (c) the Appeal Tribunal is satisfied that the benefits of earlier consideration by the Supreme Court outweigh the benefits of consideration by the Court of Appeal.
(6) No appeal lies against the grant or refusal of a certificate under subsection (1).
Amendments (Textual)
F105. Ss. 37. ZA-37. ZC inserted (8.8.2016) by Criminal Justice and Courts Act 2015 (c. 2), ss. 65, 95. (1); S.I. 2016/717, art. 3. (b) (with art. 5)

37. ZBAppeals to Supreme Court: permission to appeal

(1) If the Appeal Tribunal grants a certificate under section 37. ZA in relation to any proceedings, a party to those proceedings may apply to the Supreme Court for permission to appeal directly to the Supreme Court.
(2) An application under subsection (1) must be made—
 (a) within one month from the date on which the certificate is granted, or
 (b) within such time as the Supreme Court may allow in a particular case.
(3) If on such an application it appears to the Supreme Court to be expedient to do so, the Supreme Court may grant permission for such an appeal.
(4) If permission is granted under this section—
 (a) no appeal from the decision or order to which the certificate relates lies to the Court of Appeal, but
 (b) an appeal lies from that decision or order to the Supreme Court.
(5) An application under subsection (1) is to be determined without a hearing.
(6) Subject to subsection (4), no appeal lies to the Court of Appeal from a decision or order of the Appeal Tribunal in respect of which a certificate is granted under section 37. ZA until—
 (a) the time within which an application can be made under subsection (1) has expired, and
 (b) where such an application is made, that application has been determined in accordance with this section.
Amendments (Textual)
F105. Ss. 37. ZA-37. ZC inserted (8.8.2016) by Criminal Justice and Courts Act 2015 (c. 2), ss. 65, 95. (1); S.I. 2016/717, art. 3. (b) (with art. 5)

37. ZCAppeals to Supreme Court: exclusions

(1) No certificate may be granted under section 37. ZA in respect of a decision or order of the Appeal Tribunal in any proceedings where, by virtue of any enactment (other than sections 37. ZA and 37. ZB), no appeal would lie from that decision or order of the Appeal Tribunal to the Court of Appeal, with or without the leave or permission of the Appeal Tribunal or the Court of Appeal.
(2) No certificate may be granted under section 37. ZA in respect of a decision or order of the Appeal Tribunal in any proceedings where, by virtue of any enactment, no appeal would lie from a decision of the Court of Appeal on that decision or order of the Appeal Tribunal to the Supreme Court, with or without the leave or permission of the Court of Appeal or the Supreme Court.
(3) Where no appeal would lie to the Court of Appeal from the decision or order of the Appeal Tribunal except with the leave or permission of the Appeal Tribunal or the Court of Appeal, no certificate may be granted under section 37. ZA in respect of a decision or order of the Appeal Tribunal unless it appears to the Appeal Tribunal that it would be a proper case for granting leave or permission to appeal to the Court of Appeal.
(4) No certificate may be granted under section 37. ZA where the decision or order of the Appeal Tribunal is made in the exercise of its jurisdiction to punish for contempt.]
Amendments (Textual)
F105. Ss. 37. ZA-37. ZC inserted (8.8.2016) by Criminal Justice and Courts Act 2015 (c. 2), ss. 65, 95. (1); S.I. 2016/717, art. 3. (b) (with art. 5)

PART 2A Financial penalties for failure to pay sums ordered to be paid or settlement sums

[F1. PART 2. AFinancial penalties for failure to pay sums ordered to be paid or settlement sums

Amendments (Textual)
F1. Pt. 2. A inserted (6.4.2016) by Small Business, Enterprise and Employment Act 2015 (c. 26), ss. 150. (2), 164. (1) (with s. 150. (8)); S.I. 2016/321, reg. 3. (d)

37. ASums to which financial penalty can relate

(1) This section has effect for the purposes of this Part.
(2) "Financial award"—
   (a) means a sum of money (or, if more than one, the sums of money) ordered by an employment tribunal on a claim involving an employer and a worker, or on a relevant appeal, to be paid by the employer to the worker, and
   (b) includes—
(i) any sum (a "costs sum") required to be paid in accordance with an order in respect of costs or expenses which relate to proceedings on, or preparation time relating to, the claim or a relevant appeal, and
(ii) in a case to which section 16 applies, a sum ordered to be paid to the Secretary of State under that section.
(3) Subsection (2)(b)(i) applies irrespective of when the order was made or the amount of the costs sum was determined.
(4) "Settlement sum" means a sum payable by an employer to a worker under the terms of a settlement in respect of which a certificate has been issued under section 19. A(1).

(5) "Relevant sum" means—
　(a) a financial award, or
　(b) a settlement sum.
(6) "Relevant appeal", in relation to a financial award, means an appeal against—
　(a) the decision on the claim to which it relates,
　(b) a decision to make, or not to make, an order in respect of a financial award (including any costs sum) on the claim,
　(c) the amount of any such award, or
　(d) any decision made on an appeal within paragraphs (a) to (c) or this paragraph.
(7) Sections 37. B to 37. D apply for the purposes of calculating the unpaid amount on any day of a relevant sum.

37. BFinancial award: unpaid amount

(1) In the case of a financial award, the unpaid amount on any day means the amount outstanding immediately before that day in respect of—
　(a) the initial amount of the financial award (see subsection (2)), and
　(b) interest payable in respect of the financial award by virtue of section 14.
(2) The initial amount of a financial award is—
　(a) in a case to which section 16 applies, the monetary award within the meaning of that section (see section 17. (3)), together with any costs sum, and
　(b) in any other case, the sum or sums of money ordered to be paid (including any costs sum).
(3) An amount in respect of a financial award is not to be regarded as outstanding—
　(a) when the worker could make an application for an order for a costs sum in relation to—
(i) proceedings on the claim to which the financial award relates,
(ii) proceedings on a relevant appeal,
　(b) when the worker has made such an application but the application has not been withdrawn or finally determined,
　(c) when the employer or worker could appeal against—
(i) the decision on the claim to which it relates,
(ii) a decision to make, or not to make, a financial award (including any costs sum) on the claim,
(iii) the amount of any such award, or
(iv) any decision made on an appeal within sub-paragraphs (i) to (iii) or this sub-paragraph,
but has not done so, or
　(d) when the employer or worker has made such an appeal but the appeal has not been withdrawn or finally determined.

37. CSettlement sum: unpaid amount

(1) In the case of a settlement sum, the unpaid amount on any day means the amount outstanding immediately before that day in respect of—
　(a) the settlement sum, and
　(b) interest (if any) calculated in accordance with the settlement (within the meaning of section 19. A).
(2) Subject to section 37. D(2) and (3), an amount in respect of a settlement sum is not to be regarded as outstanding if the settlement sum is not recoverable under section 19. A(3).

37. DUnpaid amount of relevant sum: further provision

(1) Subsections (2) and (3) apply where—
　(a) a relevant sum is to be paid by instalments,

(b) any instalment is not paid on or before the day on which it is due to be paid, and
(c) a warning notice (see section 37. E) is given in consequence of the failure to pay that instalment ("the unpaid instalment").
(2) For the purposes of calculating the unpaid amount for—
(a) that warning notice, and
(b) any penalty notice given in respect of that warning notice,
any remaining instalments (whether or not yet due) are to be treated as having been due on the same day as the unpaid instalment.
(3) Accordingly, the amount outstanding in respect of the financial award or settlement sum is to be taken to be—
(a) the aggregate of—
(i) the unpaid instalment, and
(ii) any remaining instalments,
including, in the case of a settlement sum, any amount which is not recoverable under section 19. A(3) by reason only of not being due,
(b) interest on those amounts calculated in accordance with section 37. B(1)(b) or 37. C(1)(b) (and subsection (2)).
(4) Subsections (2) and (3) are not to be taken to affect the time at which any remaining instalment is due to be paid by the employer.
(5) The provisions of this Part apply where a financial award consists of two or more sums (whether or not any of them is a costs sum) which are required to be paid at different times as if—
(a) it were a relevant sum to be paid by instalments, and
(b) those sums were the instalments.
(6) Where a payment by an employer is made, or purported to be made, in respect of a relevant sum, an enforcement officer may determine whether, and to what extent, the payment is to be treated as being—
(a) in respect of that relevant sum or instead in respect of some other amount owed by the employer;
(b) in respect of the initial amount or interest on it, in the case of a payment treated as being in respect of the relevant sum.

37. EWarning notice

(1) This section applies where an enforcement officer considers that an employer who is required to pay a relevant sum has failed—
(a) in the case of a relevant sum which is to be paid by instalments, to pay an instalment on or before the day on which it is due to be paid, or
(b) in any other case, to pay the relevant sum in full on or before the day on which it is due to be paid.
(2) The officer may give the employer a notice (a "warning notice") stating the officer's intention to impose a financial penalty in respect of the relevant sum unless before a date specified in the warning notice ("the specified date") the employer has paid in full the amount so specified ("the specified amount").
This is subject to subsection (3).
(3) Where a penalty notice has previously been given in respect of the relevant sum, the officer may not give a warning notice until—
(a) 3 months have elapsed since the end of the relevant period (within the meaning of section 37. H) relating to the last penalty notice given in respect of the relevant sum, and
(b) if the relevant sum is to be paid by instalments, the last instalment has become due for payment.
(4) The specified date must be after the end of the period of 28 days beginning with the day on which the warning notice is given.

(5) The specified amount must be the unpaid amount of the relevant sum on the day on which the warning notice is given.
(6) A warning notice must identify the relevant sum and state—
  (a) how the specified amount has been calculated;
  (b) the grounds on which it is proposed to impose a penalty;
  (c) the amount of the financial penalty that would be imposed if no payment were made in respect of the relevant sum before the specified date;
  (d) that the employer may before the specified date make representations about the proposal to impose a penalty, including representations—
(i) about payments which the employer makes in respect of the relevant sum after the warning notice is given;
(ii) about the employer's ability to pay both a financial penalty and the relevant sum;
  (e) how any such representations may be made.
(7) The statement under subsection (6)(e) must include provision for allowing representations to be made by post (whether or not it also allows them to be made in any other way).
(8) If the employer pays the specified amount before the specified date, the relevant sum is to be treated for the purposes of this Part as having been paid in full.
(9) Subsection (8) is not to be taken to affect the liability of the employer to pay any increase in the unpaid amount between the date of the warning notice and the date of payment.

37. FPenalty notice

(1) This section applies where an enforcement officer—
  (a) has given a warning notice to an employer, and
  (b) is satisfied that the employer has failed to pay the specified amount in full before the specified date.
(2) The officer may give the employer a notice (a "penalty notice") requiring the employer to pay a financial penalty to the Secretary of State.
(3) A penalty notice must identify the relevant sum and state—
  (a) the grounds on which the penalty notice is given;
  (b) the unpaid amount of the relevant sum on the specified date and how it has been calculated;
  (c) the amount of the financial penalty (see subsections (4) to (6));
  (d) how the penalty must be paid;
  (e) the period within which the penalty must be paid;
  (f) how the employer may pay a reduced penalty instead of the financial penalty;
  (g) the amount of the reduced penalty (see subsection (8));
  (h) how the employer may appeal against the penalty notice;
  (i) the consequences of non-payment.
(4) Subject to subsections (5) and (6), the amount of the financial penalty is 50% of the unpaid amount of the relevant sum on the specified date.
(5) If the unpaid amount on the specified date is less than £200, the amount of the penalty is £100.
(6) If the unpaid amount on the specified date is more than £10,000, the amount of the financial penalty is £5,000.
(7) The period specified under subsection (3)(e) must be a period of not less than 28 days beginning with the day on which the penalty notice is given.
(8) The amount of the reduced penalty is 50% of the amount of the financial penalty.
(9) Subsection (10) applies if, within the period of 14 days beginning with the day on which the penalty notice is given, the employer—
  (a) pays the unpaid amount of the relevant sum on the specified date (as stated in the notice under subsection (3)(b)), and
  (b) pays the reduced penalty to the Secretary of State.
(10) The employer is to be treated—

(a) for the purposes of this Part, as having paid the relevant sum in full, and
(b) by paying the reduced penalty, as having paid the whole of the financial penalty.
(11) Subsection (10)(a) is not to be taken to affect the liability of the employer to pay any increase in the unpaid amount of the relevant sum between the specified date and the date of payment.

37. GAppeal against penalty notice

(1) An employer to whom a penalty notice is given may, before the end of the period specified under section 37. F(3)(e) (period within which penalty must be paid), appeal against—
    (a) the penalty notice; or
    (b) the amount of the financial penalty.
(2) An appeal under subsection (1) lies to an employment tribunal.
(3) An appeal under subsection (1) may be made on one or more of the following grounds—
    (a) that the grounds stated in the penalty notice under section 37. F(3)(a) were incorrect;
    (b) that it was unreasonable for the enforcement officer to have given the notice;
    (c) that the calculation of an amount stated in the penalty notice was incorrect.
(4) On an appeal under subsection (1), an employment tribunal may—
    (a) allow the appeal and cancel the penalty notice;
    (b) in the case of an appeal made on the ground that the calculation of an amount stated in the penalty notice was incorrect, allow the appeal and substitute the correct amount for the amount stated in the penalty notice;
    (c) dismiss the appeal.
(5) Where an employer has made an appeal under subsection (1), the penalty notice is not enforceable until the appeal has been withdrawn or finally determined.

37. HInterest and recovery

(1) This section applies if all or part of a financial penalty which an employer is required by a penalty notice to pay is unpaid at the end of the relevant period.
(2) The relevant period is—
    (a) if no appeal is made under section 37. G(1) relating to the penalty notice, the period specified in the penalty notice under section 37. F(3)(e);
    (b) if such an appeal is made, the period ending when the appeal is withdrawn or finally determined.
(3) The outstanding amount of the financial penalty for the time being carries interest—
    (a) at the rate that, on the last day of the relevant period, was specified in section 17 of the Judgments Act 1838,
    (b) from the end of the relevant period until the time when the amount of interest calculated under this subsection equals the amount of the financial penalty,
(and does not also carry interest as a judgment debt under that section).
(4) The outstanding amount of a penalty and any interest is recoverable—
    (a) in England and Wales, if the county court so orders, under section 85 of the County Courts Act 1984 or otherwise as if the sum were payable under an order of the county court;
    (b) in Scotland, by diligence as if the penalty notice were an extract registered decree arbitral bearing a warrant for execution issued by the sheriff court of any sheriffdom in Scotland.
(5) Any amount received by the Secretary of State under this Part is to be paid into the Consolidated Fund.

37. IWithdrawal of warning notice

(1) Where—

(a) a warning notice has been given (and not already withdrawn),
(b) it appears to an enforcement officer that—
(i) the notice incorrectly omits any statement or is incorrect in any particular, or
(ii) the warning notice was given in contravention of section 37. E(3), and
(c) if a penalty notice has been given in relation to the warning notice, any appeal made under section 37. G(1) has not been determined,
the officer may withdraw the warning notice by giving notice of withdrawal to the employer.
(2) Where a warning notice is withdrawn, no penalty notice may be given in relation to it.
(3) Where a warning notice is withdrawn after a penalty notice has been given in relation to it—
(a) the penalty notice ceases to have effect;
(b) any sum paid by or recovered from the employer by way of financial penalty payable under the penalty notice must be repaid to the employer with interest at the appropriate rate running from the date when the sum was paid or recovered;
(c) any appeal under section 37. G(1) relating to the penalty notice must be dismissed.
(4) In subsection (3)(b), the appropriate rate means the rate that, on the date the sum was paid or recovered, was specified in section 17 of the Judgments Act 1838.
(5) A notice of withdrawal under this section must indicate the effect of the withdrawal (but a failure to do so does not make the notice of withdrawal ineffective).
(6) Withdrawal of a warning notice relating to a relevant sum does not preclude a further warning notice being given in relation to that sum (subject to section 37. E(3)).

37. JWithdrawal of penalty notice

(1) Where—
(a) a penalty notice has been given (and not already withdrawn or cancelled), and
(b) it appears to an enforcement officer that—
(i) the notice incorrectly omits any statement required by section 37. F(3), or
(ii) any statement so required is incorrect in any particular,
the officer may withdraw it by giving notice of the withdrawal to the employer.
(2) Where a penalty notice is withdrawn and no replacement penalty notice is given in accordance with section 37. K—
(a) any sum paid by or recovered from the employer by way of financial penalty payable under the notice must be repaid to the employer with interest at the appropriate rate running from the date when the sum was paid or recovered;
(b) any appeal under section 37. G(1) relating to the penalty notice must be dismissed.
(3) In a case where subsection (2) applies, the notice of withdrawal must indicate the effect of that subsection (but a failure to do so does not make the withdrawal ineffective).
(4) In subsection (2)(a), "the appropriate rate" means the rate that, on the date the sum was paid or recovered, was specified in section 17 of the Judgments Act 1838.

37. KReplacement penalty notice

(1) Where an enforcement officer—
(a) withdraws a penalty notice ("the original penalty notice") under section 37. J, and
(b) is satisfied that the employer failed to pay the specified amount in full before the specified date in accordance with the warning notice in relation to which the original penalty notice was given,
the officer may at the same time give another penalty notice in relation to the warning notice ("the replacement penalty notice").
(2) The replacement penalty notice must—
(a) indicate the differences between it and the original penalty notice that the enforcement officer reasonably considers material, and

(b) indicate the effect of section 37. L.
(3) Failure to comply with subsection (2) does not make the replacement penalty notice ineffective.
(4) Where a replacement penalty notice is withdrawn under section 37. J, no further replacement penalty notice may be given under subsection (1) pursuant to the withdrawal.
(5) Nothing in this section affects any power that arises apart from this section to give a penalty notice.

37. LEffect of replacement penalty notice

(1) This section applies where a penalty notice is withdrawn under section 37. J and a replacement penalty notice is given in accordance with section 37. K.
(2) If an appeal relating to the original penalty notice has been made under section 37. G(1) and has not been withdrawn or finally determined before the time when that notice is withdrawn—
   (a) the appeal ("the earlier appeal") is to have effect after that time as if it were against the replacement penalty notice, and
   (b) the employer may exercise the right under section 37. G to appeal against the replacement penalty notice only after withdrawing the earlier appeal.
(3) If a sum was paid by or recovered from the employer by way of financial penalty under the original penalty notice—
   (a) an amount equal to that sum (or, if more than one, the total of those sums) is to be treated as having been paid in respect of the replacement penalty notice, and
   (b) any amount by which that sum (or total) exceeds the amount of the financial penalty payable under the replacement penalty notice must be repaid to the employer with interest at the appropriate rate running from the date when the sum (or, if more than one, the first of them) was paid or recovered.
(4) In subsection (3)(b) "the appropriate rate" means the rate that, on the date mentioned in that provision, was specified in section 17 of the Judgments Act 1838.

37. MEnforcement officers

The Secretary of State may appoint or authorise persons to act as enforcement officers for the purposes of this Part.

37. NPower to amend Part 2. A

(1) The Secretary of State may by regulations—
   (a) amend subsection (5) or (6) of section 37. F by substituting a different amount;
   (b) amend subsection (4) or (8) of that section by substituting a different percentage;
   (c) amend section 37. E(4) or 37. F(7) or (9) by substituting a different number of days.
(2) Any provision that could be made by regulations under this section may instead be included in an order under section 12. A(12).

37. OModification in particular cases

(1) The Secretary of State may by regulations make provision for this Part to apply with modifications in cases where—
   (a) two or more financial awards were made against an employer on claims relating to different workers that were considered together by an employment tribunal, or
   (b) settlement sums are payable by an employer under two or more settlements in cases dealt with together by a conciliation officer.

(2) Regulations under subsection (1) may in particular provide for any provision of this Part to apply as if any such financial awards or settlement sums, taken together, were a single relevant sum.
(3) The Secretary of State may by regulations make provision for this Part to apply with modifications in cases where a financial award has been made against an employer but is not regarded as outstanding by virtue only of the fact that an application for an order for a costs sum has not been finally determined (or any appeal within section 37. B(3)(c) so far as relating to the application could still be made or has not been withdrawn or finally determined).
(4) Regulations under subsection (3) may in particular provide—
   (a) for any provision of this Part to apply, or to apply if the enforcement officer so determines, as if the application had not been, and could not be, made;
   (b) for any costs sum the amount of which is subsequently determined, or the order for which is subsequently made, to be treated for the purposes of this Part as a separate relevant sum.

37. PGiving of notices

(1) For the purposes of section 7 of the Interpretation Act 1978 in its application to this Part, the proper address of an employer is—
   (a) if the employer has notified an enforcement officer of an address at which the employer is willing to accept notices, that address;
   (b) otherwise—
(i) in the case of a body corporate, the address of the body's registered or principal office;
(ii) in the case of a partnership or an unincorporated body or association, the principal office of the partnership, body or association;
(iii) in any other case, the last known address of the person in question.
(2) In the case of—
   (a) a body corporate registered outside the United Kingdom,
   (b) a partnership carrying on business outside the United Kingdom, or
   (c) an unincorporated body or association with offices outside the United Kingdom,
the references in subsection (1) to its principal office include references to its principal office within the United Kingdom (if any).

37. QFinancial penalties for non-payment: interpretation

(1) In this Part, the following terms have the following meanings—
"claim"—
   - means anything that is referred to in the relevant legislation as a claim, a complaint or a reference, other than a reference made by virtue of section 122. (2) or 128. (2) of the Equality Act 2010 (reference by court of question about a non-discrimination or equality rule etc), and
   - also includes an application, under regulations made under section 45 of the Employment Act 2002, for a declaration that a person is a permanent employee;
"costs sum" has the meaning given by section 37. A;
"employer" has the same meaning as in section 12. A;
"enforcement officer" means a person appointed or authorised to act under section 37. M;
"financial award" has the meaning given by section 37. A;
"penalty notice" has the meaning given by section 37. F;
"relevant appeal" has the meaning given by section 37. A;
"relevant sum" has the meaning given by section 37. A;
"settlement sum" has the meaning given by section 37. A;
"specified amount" and "specified date", in relation to a warning notice or a penalty notice given in relation to it, have the meanings given by section 37. E(2);
"unpaid amount"—

- in relation to a financial award, has the meaning given by section 37. B;
- in relation to a settlement sum, has the meaning given by section 37. C;
subject, in each case, to section 37. D;
"warning notice" has the meaning given by section 37. E(2);
"worker" has the same meaning as in section 12. A.
(2) References in this Part to an employer, in relation to a warning notice or penalty notice, are to the person to whom the notice is given (whether or not the person is an employer at the time in question).
(3) For the purposes of this Part a relevant sum is to be regarded as having been paid in full when the amount unpaid in respect of that sum on the date of payment has been paid.
(4) For the purposes of this Part, a penalty notice is given in relation to a warning notice if it is given as the result of a failure by the employer to pay the specified amount before the specified date.
(5) The Secretary of State may by regulations amend this section so as to alter the meaning of "claim".
(6) Any provision that could be made by regulations under subsection (5) may instead be included in an order under section 12. A(12).]

Power to amend Part 2A

[F137. NPower to amend Part 2. A

(1) The Secretary of State may by regulations—
   (a) amend subsection (5) or (6) of section 37. F by substituting a different amount;
   (b) amend subsection (4) or (8) of that section by substituting a different percentage;
   (c) amend section 37. E(4) or 37. F(7) or (9) by substituting a different number of days.
(2) Any provision that could be made by regulations under this section may instead be included in an order under section 12. A(12).]
Amendments (Textual)
F1. Pt. 2. A inserted (6.4.2016) by Small Business, Enterprise and Employment Act 2015 (c. 26), ss. 150. (2), 164. (1) (with s. 150. (8)); S.I. 2016/321, reg. 3. (d)

Part III Supplementary

Part III Supplementary

38 Crown employment.

(1) This Act has effect in relation to Crown employment and persons in Crown employment as it has effect in relation to other employment and other employees.
(2) In this Act "Crown employment" means employment under or for the purposes of a government department or any officer or body exercising on behalf of the Crown functions conferred by a statutory provision.
(3) For the purposes of the application of this Act in relation to Crown employment in accordance with subsection (1)—
   (a) references to an employee shall be construed as references to a person in Crown employment, and

(b) references to a contract of employment shall be construed as references to the terms of employment of a person in Crown employment.
(4) Subsection (1) applies to—
(a) service as a member of the naval, military or air forces of the Crown, and
(b) employment by an association established for the purposes of Part XI of the M1. Reserve Forces Act 1996;
but Her Majesty may by Order in Council make any provision of this Act apply to service as a member of the naval, military or air forces of the Crown subject to such exceptions and modifications as may be specified in the Order in Council.
Marginal Citations
M11996 c. 14.

39 Parliamentary staff.

(1) This Act has effect in relation to employment as a relevant member of the House of Lords staff or a relevant member of the House of Commons staff as it has effect in relation to other employment.
(2) Nothing in any rule of law or the law or practice of Parliament prevents a relevant member of the House of Lords staff or a relevant member of the House of Commons staff from bringing before an [F1employment tribunal] proceedings of any description which could be brought before such a tribunal by a person who is not a relevant member of the House of Lords staff or a relevant member of the House of Commons staff.
(3) For the purposes of the application of this Act in relation to a relevant member of the House of Commons staff—
(a) references to an employee shall be construed as references to a relevant member of the House of Commons staff, and
(b) references to a contract of employment shall be construed as including references to the terms of employment of a relevant member of the House of Commons staff.
(4) In this Act "relevant member of the House of Lords staff" means any person who is employed under a contract of employment with the Corporate Officer of the House of Lords.
(5) In this Act "relevant member of the House of Commons staff" has the same meaning as in section 195 of the M2. Employment Rights Act 1996; and (subject to an Order in Council under subsection (12) of that section)—
(a) subsections (6) and (7) of that section have effect for determining who is the employer of a relevant member of the House of Commons staff for the purposes of this Act, and
(b) subsection (8) of that section applies in relation to proceedings brought by virtue of this section.
Amendments (Textual)
F1. Words in s. 39. (2) substituted (1.8.1998) by 1998 c. 8, s. 1. (2)(a) (with s. 16. (2)); S.I. 1998/1658, art. 2. (1), Sch. 1
Marginal Citations
M21996 c. 18.

General

40 Power to amend Act.

(1) The Secretary of State [F2and the Lord Chancellor, acting jointly,] may by order—
(a) provide that any provision of this Act to which this section applies and which is specified in the order shall not apply to persons, or to employments, of such classes as may be prescribed in

the order, or

(b) provide that any provision of this Act to which this section applies shall apply to persons or employments of such classes as may be prescribed in the order subject to such exceptions and modifications as may be so prescribed.

(2) This section applies to sections 3, 8, 16 and 17 F3....

Amendments (Textual)

F2. Words in s. 40. (1) inserted (1.12.2007) by Tribunals, Courts and Enforcement Act 2007 (c. 15), ss. 48. (1), 148, Sch. 8 para. 38; S.I. 2007/2709, art. 4

F3. Words in s. 40. (2) omitted (6.4.2014) by virtue of Enterprise and Regulatory Reform Act 2013 (c. 24), s. 103. (3), Sch. 1 para. 8; S.I. 2014/253, art. 3. (f)

41 Orders, regulations and rules.

(1) Any power conferred by this Act on a Minister of the Crown to make an order, and any power conferred by this Act to make regulations or rules, is exercisable by statutory instrument.

(2) No recommendation shall be made to Her Majesty to make an Order in Council under section 38. (4), F4... no order shall be made under section 3, 4. (4) [F5 or (6. D)][F6, 12. A(12)][F7, 28. (5)] or 40, [F8 and no regulations are to be made under section 37. N, 37. O or 37. Q(5),] unless a draft of the Order in Council[F9, order or regulations] has been laid before Parliament and approved by a resolution of each House of Parliament.

(3) A statutory instrument containing—

(a) an order made by a Minister of the Crown under any other provision of this Act except Part II of Schedule 2, or

(b) [F10any other regulations] or rules made under this Act,

is subject to annulment in pursuance of a resolution of either House of Parliament.

(4) Any power conferred by this Act which is exercisable by statutory instrument includes power to make such incidental, supplementary or transitional provision as appears to the Minister exercising the power to be necessary or expedient.

Amendments (Textual)

F4. Word in s. 41. (2) omitted (6.4.2016) by virtue of Small Business, Enterprise and Employment Act 2015 (c. 26), ss. 150. (5)(a), 164. (1) (with s. 150. (8)); S.I. 2016/321, reg. 3. (d)

F5. Words in s. 41. (2) inserted (25.4.2013 for specified purposes) by Enterprise and Regulatory Reform Act 2013 (c. 24), ss. 11. (2), 103. (1)(i)(3)

F6. Word in s. 41. (2) inserted (6.4.2014) by Enterprise and Regulatory Reform Act 2013 (c. 24), s. 103. (3), Sch. 3 para. 4 (with s. 24. (5), Sch. 3 para. 4. (2)); S.I. 2014/253, art. 3. (h)

F7. Word in s. 41. (2) inserted (25.4.2013 for specified purposes) by Enterprise and Regulatory Reform Act 2013 (c. 24), ss. 12. (4), 103. (1)(i)(2) (with s. 24. (2))

F8. Words in s. 41. (2) inserted (6.4.2016) by Small Business, Enterprise and Employment Act 2015 (c. 26), ss. 150. (5)(b), 164. (1) (with s. 150. (8)); S.I. 2016/321, reg. 3. (d)

F9. Words in s. 41. (2) substituted (6.4.2016) by Small Business, Enterprise and Employment Act 2015 (c. 26), ss. 150. (5)(c), 164. (1) (with s. 150. (8)); S.I. 2016/321, reg. 3. (d)

F10. Words in s. 41. (3)(b) substituted (6.4.2016) by Small Business, Enterprise and Employment Act 2015 (c. 26), ss. 150. (5)(c), 164. (1) (with s. 150. (8)); S.I. 2016/321, reg. 3. (d)

42 Interpretation.

(1) In this Act [F11 (except where otherwise expressly provided)] —

[F12"ACAS" means the Advisory, Conciliation and Arbitration Service,]

"the Appeal Tribunal" means the Employment Appeal Tribunal,

"Appeal Tribunal procedure rules" shall be construed in accordance with section 30. (1),

"appointed member" shall be construed in accordance with section 22. (1)(c),

[F13"Certification Officer" shall be construed in accordance with section 254 of the Trade Union and Labour Relations (Consolidation) Act 1992,]

"conciliation officer" means an officer designated by [F14. ACAS] under section 211 of the M3. Trade Union and Labour Relations (Consolidation) Act 1992,

"contract of employment" means a contract of service or apprenticeship, whether express or implied, and (if it is express) whether oral or in writing,

"employee" means an individual who has entered into or works under (or, where the employment has ceased, worked under) a contract of employment,

"employer", in relation to an employee, means the person by whom the employee is (or, where the employment has ceased, was) employed,

"employers' association" has the same meaning as in the Trade Union and Labour Relations (Consolidation) Act 1992,

"employment" means employment under a contract of employment and "employed" shall be construed accordingly,

" [F15employment tribunal] procedure regulations" shall be construed in accordance with section 7. (1),

[F16"representative" shall be construed in accordance with section 6. (1) (in Part 1) or section 29. (1) (in Part 2),]

"statutory provision" means a provision, whether of a general or a special nature, contained in, or in any document made or issued under, any Act, whether of a general or special nature,

"successor", in relation to the employer of an employee, means (subject to subsection (2)) a person who in consequence of a change occurring (whether by virtue of a sale or other disposition or by operation of law) in the ownership of the undertaking, or of the part of the undertaking, for the purposes of which the employee was employed, has become the owner of the undertaking or part, and

"trade union" has the meaning given by section 1 of the Trade Union and Labour Relations (Consolidation) Act 1992.

(2) The definition of "successor" in subsection (1) has effect (subject to the necessary modifications) in relation to a case where—

(a) the person by whom an undertaking or part of an undertaking is owned immediately before a change is one of the persons by whom (whether as partners, trustees or otherwise) it is owned immediately after the change, or

(b) the persons by whom an undertaking or part of an undertaking is owned immediately before a change (whether as partners, trustees or otherwise) include the persons by whom, or include one or more of the persons by whom, it is owned immediately after the change,

as it has effect where the previous owner and the new owner are wholly different persons.

(3) For the purposes of this Act any two employers shall be treated as associated if—

(a) one is a company of which the other (directly or indirectly) has control, or

(b) both are companies of which a third person (directly or indirectly) has control;

and "associated employer" shall be construed accordingly.

Amendments (Textual)

F11. Words in s. 42. (1) inserted (6.4.2016) by Small Business, Enterprise and Employment Act 2015 (c. 26), ss. 150. (6), 164. (1) (with s. 150. (8)); S.I. 2016/321, reg. 3. (d)

F12. Words in s. 42. (1) inserted (6.4.2014) by Enterprise and Regulatory Reform Act 2013 (c. 24), s. 103. (3), Sch. 1 para. 9. (a); S.I. 2014/253, art. 3. (f)

F13. S. 42. (1): definition of "Certification Officer" inserted (6.4.2005) by Employment Relations Act 2004 (c. 24), ss. 49. (8), 59; S. I. 2005/872, art. 4, Sch. (with arts. 5-21)

F14. Words in s. 42. (1) substituted (6.4.2014) by Enterprise and Regulatory Reform Act 2013 (c. 24), s. 103. (3), Sch. 1 para. 9. (b); S.I. 2014/253, art. 3. (f)

F15. Words in s. 42. (1) substituted (1.8.1998) by 1998 c. 8, s. 1. (2)(a) (with s. 16. (2)); S.I. 1998/1658, art. 2. (1), Sch. 1

F16. Words in s. 42. (1) inserted (25.6.2013) by Enterprise and Regulatory Reform Act 2013 (c. 24), ss. 21. (4), 103. (2)

Marginal Citations

M31992 c. 52.

Final provisions

43 Consequential amendments.

Schedule 1 (consequential amendments) shall have effect.

44 Transitionals, savings and transitory provisions.

Schedule 2 (transitional provisions, savings and transitory provisions) shall have effect.

45 Repeals and revocations.

The enactments specified in Part I of Schedule 3 are repealed, and the instruments specified in Part II of that Schedule are revoked, to the extent specified in the third column of that Schedule.

46 Commencement.

This Act shall come into force at the end of the period of three months beginning with the day on which it is passed.

47 Extent.

This Act does not extend to Northern Ireland.

48 Short title.

This Act may be cited as [F17the Employment Tribunals Act 1996].
Amendments (Textual)
F17. Words in s. 48 substituted (1.8.1998) by 1998 c. 8, s. 1. (2)(c) (with s. 16. (2)); S.I. 1998/1658, art. 2. (1), Sch. 1

Schedules

Schedule 1. Consequential amendments

Section 43.

The Transport Act 1968 (c.73)

1. Section 135. (4)(b) of the Transport Act 1968 shall continue to have effect with the substitution (originally made by paragraph 6 of Schedule 16 to the Employment Protection (Consolidation) Act 1978) of " an [F1employment tribunal] " for the words from "a tribunal" to the end.
Amendments (Textual)

F1. Words in Sch. 1 para. 1 substituted (1.8.1998) by 1998 c. 8, s. 1. (2)(a) (with s. 16. (2)); S.I. 1998/1658, art. 2. (1), Sch. 1

The Transport Holding Company Act 1972 (c.14)

2. Section 2 of the Transport Holding Company Act 1972 shall continue to have effect with the substitution (originally made by paragraph 13 of Schedule 16 to the Employment Protection (Consolidation) Act 1978) of " an [F2employment tribunal] " for—
(a) in subsection (3)(c), the words from "a tribunal" to the end, and
(b) in subsection (7), "a tribunal established under section 12 of the Industrial Training Act 1964".
Amendments (Textual)
F2. Words in Sch. 1 para. 2 substituted (1.8.1998) by 1998 c. 8, s. 1. (2)(a) (with s. 16. (2)); S.I. 1998/1658, art. 2. (1), Sch. 1

The Sex Discrimination Act 1975 (c.65)

3. F3. . . . .
Amendments (Textual)
F3. Sch. 1 para. 3 repealed (1.10.2007) by Equality Act 2006 (c. 3), ss. 91, 93, Sch. 4 (with s. 92); S.I. 2007/2603, art. 2 (subject to art. 3)

The Race Relations Act 1976 (c.74)

4. (1)The Race Relations Act 1976 is amended as follows.
(2) In section 56. (6), for "paragraph 6. A of Schedule 9 to the Employment Protection (Consolidation) Act 1978" substitute " section 14 of [F4the Employment Tribunals Act 1996] ".
(3) F5. . . . .
Amendments (Textual)
F4. Words in Sch. 1 para. 4 substituted (1.8.1998) by 1998 c. 8, s. 1. (2)(b)(c) (with s. 16. (2)); S.I. 1998/1658, art. 2. (1), Sch. 1
F5. Sch. 1 para. 4. (3) repealed (1.10.2007) by Equality Act 2006 (c. 3), ss. 91, 93, Sch. 4 (with s. 92); S.I. 2007/2603, art. 2 (subject to art. 3)

The Aircraft and Shipbuilding Industries Act 1977 (c.3)

5. In the Aircraft and Shipbuilding Industries Act 1977—
(a) section 49. (10), and
(b) section 50. (3)(b),
shall continue to have effect with the substitution (originally made by paragraph 28 of Schedule 16 to the Employment Protection (Consolidation) Act 1978) of " an [F6employment tribunal] or, as the case may require, a tribunal established under " for "a tribunal established under section 12 of the Industrial Training Act 1964 or, as the case may require".
Amendments (Textual)
F6. Words in Sch. 1 para. 5 substituted (1.8.1998) by 1998 c. 8, s. 1. (2)(a) (with s. 16. (2)); S.I. 1998/1658, art. 2. (1), Sch. 1

The Judicial Pensions Act 1981 (c.20)

6. In section 12. (1) of the Judicial Pensions Act 1981, for "section 128 of the Employment Protection (Consolidation) Act 1978" substitute " section 1. (1) of [F7the Employment Tribunals Act 1996] ".

Amendments (Textual)
F7. Words in Sch. 1 para. 6 substituted (1.8.1998) by 1998 c. 8, s. 1. (2)(c) (with s. 16. (2)); S.I. 1998/1658, art. 2. (1), Sch. 1

The Social Security Administration Act 1992 (c.5)

[F87. In section 58. (4) of the Social Security Administration Act 1992, for "section 132 of the Employment Protection (Consolidation) Act 1978" substitute " section 16 of [F9the Employment Tribunals Act 1996] ".]
Amendments (Textual)
F8. Sch. 1 para. 7 repealed (29.11.1999) by 1998 c. 14, s. 86. (2), Sch. 8; S.I 1999/3178, art. 2 and subject to transitional provisions in Schs. 21-23)
F9. Words in Sch. 1 para. 7 substituted (1.8.1998) by 1998 c. 8, s. 1. (2)(c) (with s. 16. (2)); S.I. 1998/1658, art. 2. (1), Sch. 1

The Trade Union and Labour Relations (Consolidation) Act 1992 (c.52)

8. In section 288 of the Trade Union and Labour Relations (Consolidation) Act 1992—
(a) in subsection (2), for paragraphs (a) and (b) substitute " section 18 of [F10the Employment Tribunals Act 1996] (conciliation) ", and
(b) in subsection (2. A), for "section 290" substitute " subsection (1)(b) of that section ".
Amendments (Textual)
F10. Words in Sch. 1 para. 8. (a) substituted (1.8.1998) by 1998 c. 8, s. 1. (2)(c) (with s. 16. (2)); S.I. 1998/1658, art. 2. (1), Sch. 1

The Tribunals and Inquiries Act 1992 (c.53)

9. (1)The Tribunals and Inquiries Act 1992 is amended as follows.
(2) In section 11. (2), for "section 136. (1) of the Employment Protection (Consolidation) Act 1978" substitute " section 21. (1) of [F11the Employment Tribunals Act 1996] ".
(3) In Schedule 1—
(a) in Part I, in paragraph 16, and
(b) in Part II, in paragraph 51,
for "section 128 of the Employment Protection (Consolidation) Act 1978 (c. 44)" substitute " section 1. (1) of [F11the Employment Tribunals Act 1996] (c. 17) ".
Amendments (Textual)
F11. Words in Sch. 1 para. 9. (2)(3) substituted (1.8.1998) by 1998 c. 8, s. 1. (2)(c) (with s. 16. (2)); S.I. 1998/1658, art. 2. (1), Sch. 1

The Judicial Pensions and Retirement Act 1993 (c.8)

10. (1)The Judicial Pensions and Retirement Act 1993 is amended as follows.
(2) In Schedule 1, in Part II, in the entry relating to the office of chairman of [F12employment tribunals], for "section 128 of the Employment Protection (Consolidation) Act 1978" substitute " section 1. (1) of [F12the Employment Tribunals Act 1996] ".
(3) In Schedule 5—
(a) in the entry relating to the office of chairman of [F12employment tribunals], for "section 128 of the Employment Protection (Consolidation) Act 1978" substitute " section 1. (1) of [F12the Employment Tribunals Act 1996] ", and
(b) in the entry relating to the office of member of the Employment Appeal Tribunal, for "section

135. (2)(c) of the Employment Protection (Consolidation) Act 1978" substitute " section 22. (1)(c) of [F12the Employment Tribunals Act 1996] ".
(4) In paragraph 5 of Schedule 7—
(a) in sub-paragraphs (2)(g) and (5)(vii), for "section 128 of the Employment Protection (Consolidation) Act 1978" substitute " section 1. (1) of [F12the EmploymentTribunals Act 1996] ", and
(b) in sub-paragraph (7), for "section 135. (2)(c) of the Employment Protection (Consolidation) Act 1978" substitute " section 22. (1)(c) of [F12the Employment Tribunals Act 1996] ".
Amendments (Textual)
F12. Words in Sch. 1 para. 10 substituted (1.8.1998) by 1998 c. 8, s. 1. (2)(b)(c) (with s. 16. (2)); S.I. 1998/1658, art. 2. (1), Sch. 1

The Pension Schemes Act 1993 (c.48)

11. In section 181. (1) of the Pension Schemes Act 1993, in the definition of " [F13employment tribunal]", for "section 128 of the Employment Protection (Consolidation) Act 1978" substitute " section 1. (1) of [F13the Employment Tribunals Act 1996] ".
Amendments (Textual)
F13. Words in Sch. 1 para. 11 substituted (1.8.1998) by 1998 c. 8, s. 1. (2)(b)(c) (with s. 16. (2)); S.I. 1998/1658, art. 2. (1), Sch. 1

The Disability Discrimination Act 1995 (c.50)

12. (1)The Disability Discrimination Act 1995 is amended as follows.
(2) In section 8. (7), for "paragraph 6. A of Schedule 9 to the Employment Protection (Consolidation) Act 1978" substitute " section 14 of [F14the Employment Tribunals Act 1996] ".
(3) In section 9. (2)(a), for "paragraph 1 of Schedule 3" substitute " section 18 of [F14the Employment Tribunals Act 1996] ".
Amendments (Textual)
F14. Words in Sch. 1 para. 12. (2)(3) substituted (1.8.1998) by 1998 c. 8, s. 1. (2)(c) (with s. 16. (2)); S.I. 1998/1658, art. 2. (1), Sch. 1

Schedule 2. Transitional provisions, savings and transitory provisions

Section 44.

Part I Transitional provisions and savings

1. The substitution of this Act for the provisions repealed or revoked by this Act does not affect the continuity of the law.
2. Anything done, or having effect as done, (including the making of subordinate legislation) under or for the purposes of any provision repealed or revoked by this Act has effect as if done under or for the purposes of any corresponding provision of this Act.
3. Any reference (express or implied) in this Act or any other enactment, or in any instrument or document, to a provision of this Act is (so far as the context permits) to be read as (according to the context) being or including in relation to times, circumstances and purposes before the commencement of this Act a reference to the corresponding provision repealed or revoked by this Act.

4. (1)Any reference (express or implied) in any enactment, or in any instrument or document, to a provision repealed or revoked by this Act is (so far as the context permits) to be read as (according to the context) being or including in relation to times, circumstances and purposes after the commencement of this Act a reference to the corresponding provision of this Act.
(2) In particular, where a power conferred by an Act is expressed to be exercisable in relation to enactments contained in Acts passed before or in the same Session as the Act conferring the power, the power is also exercisable in relation to provisions of this Act which reproduce such enactments.
5. Paragraphs 1 to 4 have effect in place of section 17. (2) of the M1. Interpretation Act 1978 (but are without prejudice to any other provision of that Act).
Marginal Citations
M11978 c. 30.
6. The repeal by this Act of section 130 of, and Schedule 10 to, the M2. Employment Protection (Consolidation) Act 1978 (jurisdiction of referees under specified provisions to be exercised by [F1employment tribunals]) does not affect—
(a) the operation of those provisions in relation to any question which may arise after the commencement of this Act, or
(b) the continued operation of those provisions after the commencement of this Act in relation to any question which has arisen before that commencement.
Amendments (Textual)
F1. Words in Sch. 2 para. 6 substituted (1.8.1998) by 1998 c. 8, s. 1. (2)(b) (with s. 16. (2)); S.I. 1998/1658, art. 2. (1), Sch. 1
Marginal Citations
M21978 c. 44.

Part II Transitory provisions

Disability discrimination

F27. . . . .
Amendments (Textual)
F2. Sch. 2 para. 7 repealed by Equality Act 2010 (c. 15), Sch. 27 Pt 1 (as amended) (1.10.2010) by S.I. 2010/2279, art. 1. (2), Sch. 2 (see S.I. 2010/2317, art. 2)

Jobseeker's allowance

8. (1)If paragraph 2 of Schedule 2 to the M3 Jobseekers Act 1995 has not come into force before the commencement of this Act, this Act shall have effect until the relevant commencement date as if a reference to unemployment benefit were substituted for—
(a) each of the references to jobseeker's allowance in subsections (3) and (4) of section 16,
(b) the second reference to jobseeker's allowance in subsection (5) of that section,
(c) the first reference to jobseeker's allowance in subsection (1) of section 17, and
(d) the reference to jobseeker's allowance in subsection (2) of that section.
(2) The reference in sub-paragraph (1) to the relevant commencement date is a reference—
(a) if an order has been made before the commencement of this Act appointing a day after that commencement as the day on which paragraph 2 of Schedule 2 to the M4. Jobseekers Act 1995 is to come into force, to the day so appointed, and
(b) otherwise, to such day as the Secretary of State may by order appoint.
Marginal Citations
M31995 c. 18.

M41995 c. 18.

Armed forces

9. (1)If section 31 of the M5. Trade Union Reform and Employment Rights Act 1993 has not come into force before the commencement of this Act, section 38 shall have effect until the relevant commencement date as if for subsection (4) there were substituted—
"(4)Subsection (1)—
    (a) does not apply to service as a member of the naval, military or air forces of the Crown, but
    (b) does apply to employment by an association established for the purposes of Part XI of the M6. Reserve Forces Act 1996."
(2) The reference in sub-paragraph (1) to the relevant commencement date is a reference—
(a) if an order has been made before the commencement of this Act appointing a day after that commencement as the day on which section 31 of the Trade Union Reform and Employment Rights Act 1993 is to come into force, to the day so appointed, and
(b) otherwise, to such day as the Secretary of State may by order appoint.
Marginal Citations
M51993 c. 19.
M61996 c. 14.
10. (1)If Part XI of the Reserve Forces Act 1996 has not come into force before the commencement of this Act, section 38 of this Act shall have effect until the relevant commencement date as if for "Part XI of the Reserve Forces Act 1996" there were substituted " Part VI of the M7. Reserve Forces Act 1980 ".
(2) The reference in sub-paragraph (1) to the relevant commencement date is a reference—
(a) if an order has been made before the commencement of this Act appointing a day after that commencement as the day on which Part XI of the Reserve Forces Act 1996 is to come into force, to the day so appointed, and
(b) otherwise, to such day as the Secretary of State may by order appoint.
Marginal Citations
M71980 c. 9.

Schedule 3. Repeals and revocations

Section 45.

Part I Repeals

Chapter	Short title	Extent of repeal
1963 c. 2.	The Betting, Gaming and Lotteries Act 1963.	In Schedule 5A, paragraph 21.
1975 c. 65.	The Sex Discrimination Act 1975.	Section 64.
1976 c. 74.	The Race Relations Act 1976.	Section 55.
1978 c. 44.	The Employment Protection (Consolidation) Act 1978.	Section 128.
		Sections 130 to 136A.
		Section 138(7)(e).
		Section 139(1)(d).
		Section 139A(3)(a).
		Schedules 9 to 11.
		In Schedule 15, paragraph 18.
		In Schedule 16, paragraphs 3, 6, 13, 16, 20(2), 25(3) and 28.
1980 c. 30.	The Social Security Act 1980.	In Schedule 4, paragraph 13.

Citation	Act	Extent
1980 c. 42.	The Employment Act 1980.	In Schedule 1, paragraphs 16 to 18 and 26 to 29.
1981 c. 49.	The Contempt of Court Act 1981.	Section 16(6).
1981 c. 54.	The Supreme Court Act 1981.	In Schedule 5, the entry relating to the Employment Protection (Consolidation) Act 1978.
1982 c. 46.	The Employment Act 1982.	In Schedule 3, in Part I, paragraphs 7 to 9.
1986 c. 48.	The Wages Act 1986.	In Schedule 4, paragraphs 9 and 10.
1986 c. 50.	The Social Security Act 1986.	In Schedule 10, in Part II, paragraph 50.
1989 c. 38.	The Employment Act 1989.	Section 20. In Schedule 6, paragraph 26.
1992 c. 6.	The Social Security (Consequential Provisions) Act 1992.	In Schedule 2, paragraph 50.
1992 c. 52.	The Trade Union and Labour Relations (Consolidation) Act 1992.	Section 290. Section 291(2) and (3). In Schedule 2, paragraphs 19, 20, 24(1) and (2) and 25.
1993 c. 8.	The Judicial Pensions and Retirement Act 1993.	In Schedule 6, paragraph 30.
1993 c. 19.	The Trade Union Reform and Employment Rights Act 1993.	Sections 36 to 38. Sections 40 to 42. In Schedule 7, paragraphs 6 and 7. In Schedule 8, paragraphs 19, 20, 28 to 30, 86 and 87.
1993 c. 48.	The Pension Schemes Act 1993.	In Schedule 8, paragraph 11(2).
1994 c. 20.	The Sunday Trading Act 1994.	In Schedule 4, paragraph 21.
1995 c. 18.	The Jobseekers Act 1995.	In Schedule 2, paragraph 2.
1995 c. 26.	The Pensions Act 1995.	In Schedule 3, paragraphs 8 and 9.
1995 c. 50.	The Disability Discrimination Act 1995.	Section 62.
		Section 63.
		In Schedule 3, paragraph 1.
		In Schedule 6, paragraph 2.

Part II Revocations

Number	Title	Extent of revocation
S.I. 1983/1794.	The Equal Pay (Amendment) Regulations 1983.	Regulation 3(3) and (4).
S.I. 1995/2587.	The Collective Redundancies and Transfer of Undertakings (Protection of Employment) (Amendment) Regulations 1995.	Regulation 12(3).
		Regulation 13(3).
		In Regulation 14(4), the words ", and paragraph 2(2) of Schedule 9 to,".

TABLE OF DERIVATIONS

Notes:
1. This Table shows the derivation of the provisions of the consolidation.
2. The following abbreviations are used in the Table—

EP(C)A | = Employment Protection (Consolidation) Act 1978 (c.44) |
TULR(C)A | = Trade Union and Labour Relations (Consolidation) Act 1992 (c.52) |
TURERA | = Trade Union Reform and Employment Rights Act 1993 (c.19) |

Provision	Derivation
1(1)	EP(C)A s.128(1).
(2)	
2	EP(C)A s.128(1).
3(1)	EP(C)A s.131(1); TURERA s.38(a).
(2)	EP(C)A s.131(2).
(3)	EP(C)A s.131(3); TURERA s.38(b).
(4)	EP(C)A s.131(6).
(5)	EP(C)A s.131(7); TURERA s.38(e).
(6)	EP(C)A s.131(7).

4(1), (2) | EP(C)A s.128(2A), (2B); TURERA s.36(2). |
(3) | EP(C)A s.128(2C); TURERA s.36(2); Pension Schemes Act 1993 (c.48) Sch.8 para.11(2). |
(4) | EP(C)A s.128(2D); TURERA s.36(2). |
(5) | EP(C)A s.128(2F); TURERA s.36(2). |
(6), (7) | EP(C)A s.128(5), (6); TURERA s.36(3). |
5(1) | EP(C)A Sch.9 para.9; Transfer of Functions (Minister for the Civil Service and Treasury) Order 1981 (S.I. 1981/1670). |
(2) | EP(C)A Sch.9 para.10; Transfer of Functions (Minister for the Civil Service and Treasury) Order 1981 (S.I. 1981/1670); Equal Pay (Amendment) Regulations 1983 (S.I. 1983/1794) Reg.3(4). |
(3) | EP(C)A Sch.9 para.10; Transfer of Functions (Minister for the Civil Service and Treasury) Order 1981 (S.I. 1981/1670). |
6(1) | EP(C)A Sch.9 para.6. |
(2) | EP(C)A Sch.9 para.4. |
7(1) | EP(C)A Sch.9 para.1(1). |
(2) | EP(C)A s.128(4); Employment Act 1980 (c.42) Sch.1 para.16. |
(3) | EP(C)A Sch.9 para.1(2)(a) to (ga), (j); Employment Act 1980 (c.42) Sch.1 para.26; Equal Pay (Amendment) Regulations 1983 (S.I. 1983/1794) Reg.3(3); Employment Act 1989 (c.38) Sch.6 para.26. |
(4) | EP(C)A Sch.9 para.1(7); Criminal Justice Act 1982 (c.48) ss.38, 46; Equal Pay (Amendment) Regulations 1983 (S.I. 1983/1794) Reg.3(3); Criminal Procedure (Consequential Provisions) (Scotland) Act 1995 (c.40) Sch.1. |
(5) | EP(C)A Sch.9 para.1(6); TURERA s.40(3). |
(6) | EP(C)A Sch.9 para.5. |
8(1) | EP(C)A s.131(4). |
(2) | EP(C)A s.131(4A); TURERA s.38(c). |
(3) | EP(C)A s.131(5). |
(4) | EP(C)A s.131(5A); TURERA s.38(d). |
9(1) | EP(C)A Sch.9 para.1A(1); Employment Act 1989 (c.38) s.20; TURERA Sch.8 para.28(b). |
(2), (3) | EP(C)A Sch.9 para.1A(2), (3); Employment Act 1989 (c.38) s.20. |
(4) | EP(C)A Sch.9 para.1B; TURERA Sch.8 para.28(c). |
10(1) | EP(C)A Sch.9 para.1(4A); TURERA Sch.7 para.6(a). |
(2) | EP(C)A Sch.9 para.1(5); TULR(C)A Sch.3 para.1(4). |
(3) | EP(C)A ss.138(7)(e), 139(1)(d), 139A(3)(a); TURERA Sch.7 para.11. |
(4) | EP(C)A Sch.9 para.2(1); TULR(C)A Sch.2 para.24(1), (2). |
(5) | EP(C)A Sch.9 para.2(2); TURERA Sch.7 para.6(b); Collective Redundancies and Transfer of Undertakings (Protection of Employment) (Amendment) Regulations (S.I. 1995/2587) Reg.14(4). |
(6) | EP(C)A ss.138(7)(c), 139(1)(c). |
11(1) | EP(C)A Sch.9 para.1(5A); TURERA s.40(2). |
(2) to (5) | EP(C)A Sch.9 para.1(8) to (11); TURERA s.40(4). |
(6) | EP(C)A Sch.9 para.1(5A), (8); TURERA s.40(2), (4); Criminal Procedure (Consequential Provisions) (Scotland) Act 1995 (c.40) s.2(4). |
12 | Disability Discrimination Act 1995 (c.50) s.62. |
13(1) | EP(C)A Sch.9 para.1(2)(h), (i). |
(2) | EP(C)A Sch.9 para.1(4); TURERA Sch.8 para.28(a). |
14 | EP(C)A Sch.9 para.6A; Employment Act 1982 (c.46) Sch.3 Pt.I para.7. |
15(1) | EP(C)A Sch.9 para.7(1). |
(2) | EP(C)A Sch.9 para.7(2); Employment Act 1980 (c.42) Sch.1 para.27. |
(3) | EP(C)A Sch.9 para.7(3). |
16(1) | Betting, Gaming and Lotteries Act 1963 (c.2) Sch.5A para.16; EP(C)A s.132(1); TULR(C)A Sch.2 para.19; TURERA Sch.8 para.19; Sunday Trading Act 1994 (c.20) Sch.4 para.16; Deregulation and Contracting Out Act 1994 (c.40) Sch.8. |

(2) | EP(C)A s.132(2). |
(3) | EP(C)A s.132(2); Social Security Act 1986 (c.50) Sch.10 Pt.II para.50(a); Jobseekers Act 1995 (c.18) Sch.2 para.2(2). |
(4) | EP(C)A s.132(3)(a); Social Security Act 1986 (c.50) Sch.10 Pt.II para.50(b)(i); Jobseekers Act 1995 (c.18) Sch.2 para.2(2). |
(5) | EP(C)A s.132(3)(b) to (f); Social Security Act 1980 (c.30) Sch.4 para.13; Health and Social Services and Social Security Adjudications Act 1983 (c.41) Sch.8 Pt.I para.1; Social Security Act 1986 (c.50) Sch.10 Pt.II para.50(b); Jobseekers Act 1995 (c.18) Sch.2 para.2(2), (3). |
(6) | EP(C)A s.132(3)(g). |
17(1) | EP(C)A s.132(4); Social Security Act 1986 (c.50) Sch.10 Pt.II para.50(c); Social Security (Consequential Provisions) Act 1992 (c.6) Sch.2 para.50(1); Jobseekers Act 1995 (c.18) Sch.2 para.2(2), (4). |
(2) | EP(C)A s.132(5); Jobseekers Act 1995 (c.18) Sch.2 para.2(2). |
(3) | EP(C)A s.132(6). |
(4) | EP(C)A s.132(6); Jobseekers Act 1995 (c.18) Sch.2 para.2(5). |
18(1) | Betting, Gaming and Lotteries Act 1963 (c.2) Sch.5A para.21; Sex Discrimination Act 1975 (c.65) s.64(1); Race Relations Act 1976 (c.74) s.55(1); EP(C)A ss.133(1), 134(1); Employment Act 1980 (c.42) Sch.1 para.17; Wages Act 1986 (c.48) Sch.4 para.9; TULR(C)A s.290; TURERA Sch.8 paras.20, 86; Sunday Trading Act 1994 (c.20) Sch.4 para.21; Deregulation and Contracting Out Act 1994 (c.40) Sch.8; Pensions Act 1995 (c.26) Sch.3 para.8; Disability Discrimination Act 1995 (c.50) Sch.3 para.1; Collective Redundancies and Transfer of Undertakings (Protection of Employment) (Amendment) Regulations (S.I. 1995/2587) Regs.12(3), 13(3). |
(2) | Sex Discrimination Act 1975 (c.65) s.64(1); Race Relations Act 1976 (c.74) s.55(1); EP(C)A ss.133(2), (4), 134(1); Disability Discrimination Act 1995 (c.50) Sch.3 para.1(1). |
(3) | Sex Discrimination Act 1975 (c.65) s.64(2); Race Relations Act 1976 (c.74) s.55(2); EP(C)A ss.133(3), (4), 134(3); Employment Act 1980 (c.42) Sch.1 para.18; Disability Discrimination Act 1995 (c.50) Sch.3 para.1(2). |
(4) | EP(C)A s.134(2). |
(5) | EP(C)A s.134(3); Employment Act 1980 (c.42) Sch.1 para.18. |
(6) | Sex Discrimination Act 1975 (c.65) s.64(3); Race Relations Act 1976 (c.74) s.55(3); EP(C)A ss.133(5), 134(4); Disability Discrimination Act 1995 (c.50) Sch.3 para.1(3). |
(7) | Sex Discrimination Act 1975 (c.65) s.64(4); Race Relations Act 1976 (c.74) s.55(4); EP(C)A ss.133(6), 134(5); Disability Discrimination Act 1995 (c.50) Sch.3 para.1(4). |
(8) | EP(C)A s.133(7). |
19 | EP(C)A Sch.9 para.1(3). |
20(1) | EP(C)A s.135(1). |
(2) | EP(C)A Sch.11 paras.13, 14. |
(3) | EP(C)A Sch.11 para.12. |
21(1) | Betting, Gaming and Lotteries Act 1963 (c.2) Sch.5A para.16; EP(C)A s.136(1); Wages Act 1986 (c.48) Sch.4 para.10; TULR(C)A s.291(2); Sunday Trading Act 1994 (c.20) Sch.4 para.16; Deregulation and Contracting Out Act 1994 (c.40) Sch.8; Pensions Act 1995 (c.26) Sch.3 para.9; Disability Discrimination Act 1995 (c.50) Sch.6 para.2. |
(2) | EP(C)A s.136(5); TULR(C)A s.291(3). |
(3) | |
22(1) | EP(C)A s.135(2). |
(2) | EP(C)A s.135(3); TULR(C)A Sch.2 para.20. |
(3), (4) | EP(C)A s.135(4), (5). |
23(1) | EP(C)A Sch.11 para.4. |
(2) | EP(C)A Sch.11 paras.5, 6. |
(3) | EP(C)A Sch.11 para.7. |
(4) | EP(C)A Sch.11 para.9. |
(5) | EP(C)A Sch.11 para.11. |

24(1) | EP(C)A Sch.11 para.8(1). |
(2) | EP(C)A Sch.11 para.8(2); Supreme Court Act 1981 (c.54) Sch.5, entry relating to EP(C)A. |
(3) | EP(C)A Sch.11 para.10. |
25(1) | EP(C)A Sch.11 para.1. |
(2), (3) | EP(C)A Sch.11 para.2; Judicial Pensions and Retirement Act 1993 (c.8) Sch.6 para.30. |
(4) | EP(C)A Sch.11 para.3. |
26 | EP(C)A Sch.11 para.24; Transfer of Functions (Treasury and Minister for the Civil Service) Order 1995 (S.I. 1995/269). |
27(1) | EP(C)A Sch.11 para.25; Transfer of Functions (Minister for the Civil Service and Treasury) Order 1981 (S.I. 1981/1670); Transfer of Functions (Treasury and Minister for the Civil Service) Order 1995 (S.I. 1995/269). |
(2) to (4) | EP(C)A Sch.11 paras.26 to 28; Transfer of Functions (Minister for the Civil Service and Treasury) Order 1981 (S.I. 1981/1670). |
28(1) | EP(C)A Sch.11 para.15. |
(2) to (5) | EP(C)A Sch.11 para.16; TURERA s.37. |
29(1) | EP(C)A Sch.11 para.20. |
(2) | EP(C)A Sch.11 para.22(1). |
30(1) | EP(C)A Sch.11 para.17(1). |
(2) | EP(C)A Sch.11 para.18; Employment Act 1980 (c.42) Sch.1 para.28; Employment Act 1982 (c.46) Sch.3 Pt.I para.8(1); TULR(C)A Sch.2 para.25(a); TURERA Sch.7 para.7, Sch.8 paras.29, 30. |
(3) | EP(C)A Sch.11 para.17(2). |
31(1) to (6) | EP(C)A Sch.11 para.18A(1) to (6); TURERA s.41. |
(7) | EP(C)A Sch.11 para.18A(7); TURERA s.41. |
(8) | EP(C)A Sch.11 para.18A(7); TURERA s.41; Criminal Procedure (Consequential Provisions) (Scotland) Act 1995 (c.40) s.2(4). |
32(1), (2) | Disability Discrimination Act 1995 (c.50) s.63(1), (2). |
(3) to (6) | Disability Discrimination Act 1995 (c.50) ss.62(3) to (6), 63(3). |
(7) | Disability Discrimination Act 1995 (c.50) s.63(4), (5). |
(8) | Disability Discrimination Act 1995 (c.50) ss.62(7), 63(6). |
33(1) to (4) | EP(C)A s.136A(1) to (4); TURERA s.42. |
(5) | EP(C)A s.136A(6); TURERA s.42. |
34 | EP(C)A Sch.11 para.19. |
35 | EP(C)A Sch.11 para.21. |
36(1) | EP(C)A Sch.11 para.21A(1); Employment Act 1980 (c.42) Sch.1 para.29; TULR(C)A Sch.2 para.25(b). |
(2) | EP(C)A Sch.11 para.21A(2); Employment Act 1980 (c.42) Sch.1 para.29. |
(3) | EP(C)A Sch.11 para.21A(3); Employment Act 1982 (c.46) Sch.3 Pt.I para.9; TULR(C)A Sch.2 para.25(b). |
(4) | EP(C)A Sch.11 para.22(2). |
(5) | EP(C)A Sch.11 para.23(2). |
37(1), (2) | EP(C)A s.136(4). |
(3) | EP(C)A s.136A(5); TURERA s.42. |
(4) | EP(C)A s.136(4). |
38(1), (2) | EP(C)A s.138(1), (2). |
(3) | EP(C)A s.138(7)(a), (b). |
(4) | EP(C)A ss.138(3), 138A(2)(b); TURERA s.31; Reserve Forces Act 1996 (c.14) Sch.10 para.17. |
39(1) | EP(C)A ss.139(1), 139A(1); TURERA Sch.7 para.11. |
(2) | EP(C)A ss.139(2), 139A(2); TURERA Sch.7 para.11. |
(3) | EP(C)A s.139(1)(a), (b). |
(4) | EP(C)A s.139A(5); TURERA Sch.7 para.11. |
(5) | EP(C)A s.139(3) to (9). |

40(1) | EP(C)A s.149(1). |
(2) | EP(C)A s.149(2). |
41(1) | EP(C)A ss.154(1). |
(2) | EP(C)A ss.128(2E), 131(8), 138A((6), 149(4); TURERA ss.31(2), 36(2). |
(3), (4) | EP(C)A s.154(2), (3). |
42(1) |
"Appeal Tribunal" | |
"Appeal Tribunal procedure rules" | |
"appointed member" | |
"conciliation officer" | |
"contract of employment", "employee", "employer" | EP(C)A s.153(1). |
"employers' association" | EP(C)A s.153(1); TULR(C)A Sch.2 para.21(2)(a). |
"employment", "employed", "statutory provision" | EP(C)A s.153(1). |
"industrial tribunal procedure rules" | |
"successor" | EP(C)A s.153(1); TULR(C)A Sch.2 para.21(2)(d). |
"trade union" | EP(C)A s.153(1); TULR(C)A Sch.2 para.21(2)(f). |
(2) | EP(C)A s.153(4A); TULR(C)A Sch.2 para.21(3). |
(3) | EP(C)A s.153(4). |
43 | |
44 | |
45 | |
46 | |
47 | |
48 | |
Sch. 1 | |
Sch. 2 | |
Sch. 3 | |

Open Government Licence v3.0

Contains public sector information licensed under the Open Government Licence v3.0. The full licence if available at the following address:
http://www.nationalarchives.gov.uk/doc/open-government-licence/version/3/

Printed in Great Britain
by Amazon